SINGLE MINDED

PRAISE FOR SINGLE-MINDED

"*Single-Minded* delivers a timely and essential message to Christians who are single: 'Instead of walking toward marriage, walk toward Jesus.' Bob is a man of character who has written this while living this walk faithfully himself. His words are articulate, compelling, compassionate, and covered in Scripture. This book is an absolutely encouraging must-read for every unmarried Christian."

—RORY VADEN
New York Times bestselling author of *Take the Stairs*,
host of the *Eternal Life* podcast

"If you are single, spending thirty days with *Single-Minded* will most certainly wake you up, shake you up, challenge you, and lead you to a place of contentment. God brought me peace through Bob's words—a recognition of the things I knew to be true about myself, my life as a widow, and the culture in which we live. The challenges you'll find before you as you make your way through this book might even propel you toward healing you didn't know you needed."

—KELLY CORDAY
Program Director and Host at *KCBI Radio* and *Christian Nation*

"I've known Bob for years, and his hunger for truth is one of the most impressive things about him. Anchored in Scripture and fascinating anecdotes, it is hard to envision working through this and remaining unchanged. Bob gives the reader a firm and much-needed reminder—one that all too often gets lost in modern discourse—that the founder and perfecter of the Christian faith was single. The best part, though? You don't have to be single to enjoy this."

—RYAN BETHEA
Cohost and producer of *The Exorcist Files* and *Heaven Meets Earth*

"In my conversations with singles, I find many wandering without purpose, wondering about their future, or waiting for their spouse to arrive. In *Single-Minded*, Bob shares scriptural insights and stories gleaned from his own journey that provide a solid foundation for singles to build their lives upon. If you find yourself in need of getting your heart more aligned with God's, learning how to walk more godly within your relationships, or discovering more about living life fully for God's purposes, *Single-Minded* is a resource that will encourage and equip you to get there!"

—DAVE BUEHRING
Founder & President of Lionshare Leadership Group

SINGLE

MINDED

FINDING PURPOSE & STRENGTH
IN YOUR SEASON OF SINGLENESS

BOB WHEATLEY

For You, my King

My heart is overflowing with a good theme;
I recite my composition concerning the King;
My tongue is the pen of a ready writer.
—PSALM 45:1 NKJV

CONTENTS

MIND

STRENGTH

THE PAULINE ADVANTAGE

Imitate me, just as I also imitate Christ.
—1 CORINTHIANS 11:1 NKJV

I used to think Paul was ridiculous. He was God's chosen apostle, a mouthpiece to the Gentiles, yet I somehow still found him offensive. What caused me to scoff at this heralded saint? It was not the beatings, the shipwrecks, or the hardships he faced, nor was it his devotion, conversion, or capacity for love. My contempt for this man stemmed from one page of Scripture, and a teaching that I loathed to my core.

Addressing Christian believers in the church of Corinth, the apostle Paul wrote this:

> To the unmarried and the widows I say that it is good for them to remain single, as I am . . . I think that in view of the present distress it is good for a person to remain as he is. Are you bound to a wife? Do not seek to be free. Are you free from a wife? Do not seek a wife . . . I want you to be free from anxieties. The unmarried man is anxious about the things of the Lord, how to please the Lord. But the married man is anxious about worldly things, how to please his wife, and his interests are divided . . . I say this for your own benefit, not to lay any restraint upon

1

you, but to promote good order and to secure your undivided
devotion to the Lord. (1 Corinthians 7:8, 26–27, 32–34, 35)

Upon my first read, I could not believe what my eyes were seeing.
How could anyone believe that being single is better? I could not wrap
my head around that. The thought seemed so foreign, so impossible
to me, that it actually caused me to doubt my own level of faith. If
I couldn't be joyfully single, like Paul, then was my faith far weaker
than I thought it was? Was I less of a Christian if I struggled with
singleness?

But then, sure enough, my excuses came to the rescue. I knew
that Paul had navigated his entire ministry without a woman at his
side, but that didn't seem plausible for me. While I was just a man,
this man was a saint. This was Paul, a man who was called, chosen,
and set apart from the rest. The truth is, Paul had a connection to
the Lord that we cannot fathom—and all for good reason, of course.
The risen Jesus physically appeared to Paul on the Damascus road
(Acts 9). As most theologians will attest, it was Paul who had literally
seen God, face-to-face, when he was caught up into the third heaven
(2 Corinthians 12).

Those excuses gave me enough ammunition to not take Paul seriously. *Who knows, Paul? Maybe even I could forsake companionship,
sex, and the blessings of marriage if I, too, had been snatched into heaven.*

But that was not true at all. If I'm being honest, I did not want to
go deeper. I did not want to be single—let alone be single and happy!
I really just wanted a wife. I always had. But without experiencing
some sort of miraculous vision on the road to Damascus, I would not
allow Paul's words to obtrude on me.

But then everything changed.

One afternoon, I was reading a book by Eric Metaxas. The book
was called *Bonhoeffer: Pastor, Martyr, Prophet, Spy*. It told the story of a
German pastor, living during World War II under the Nazi regime. The

name of this German was Dietrich Bonhoeffer, and his testimony would change my life.

I did not want to be single—let alone be single and happy! I really just wanted a wife.

I typically consume about forty books a year. I read a lot. But I had never experienced a book like *Bonhoeffer*. Its reading was a completely unique experience for me. Like most readers, I often resonate with the book's characters in some form or fashion. It is one of the things I love most about books. Whether fiction or fact, novel or biography, I find nuggets and nuances that bind me to characters. It was C. S. Lewis who once said, "In reading great literature I become a thousand men and yet remain myself."[1] And yet, *Bonhoeffer* went deeper than that.

With nearly every word I read, I saw a clearer and clearer reflection of myself. This was a familiar routine for books, of course, but the difference was, it never stopped. Whispers and subtlety soon gave way to weirdness. Dietrich's spirit, his habits, his passions, his faults—somehow, I possessed them all.

His mind operated in black and white.

His tongue often spoke in absolutes.

His bedroom, like mine, was fit for a Spartan. Within that room, you'd find a bed, a desk, a dresser, and books. That was all Dietrich needed. He spent hours at that desk, writing away, wetting the whistle of his unceasing mind. He left no stone unturned, no question unanswered. Metaxas accused him of even "thinking about thinking."[2]

Now, just so we're clear, I am not at all saying that Dietrich was perfect. I did, however, see much of myself in him, which made this pastor especially endearing to me. As I looked around my own bedroom, what greeted me seemed quite peculiar—a bed, a desk, a dresser, and books. It, too, was spartanly clad. Much like the young Bonhoeffer, I often saw things in black and white. I also often spoke in absolutes. But at the end of the day, it was actually our birthdays that brought it all home:

February 4, 1906.

February 4, 1992.

I told you that things got weird.

As I continued to read about my "long-lost twin," I was greatly encouraged by the path that he followed. My euphoria lasted for hundreds of pages. In this young, fiery pastor, I had found a more righteous, more accomplished, more intelligent version of me. Though separated by time and a great many miles, I had found my new hero of the faith.

But then, the game turned sour for me. I eventually came across a different quote, this one by another World War II pastor. His name was Theodor Heckel, and he was a mentor and friend in Bonhoeffer's circle. He actually found Dietrich to be "quite outstanding,"[3] and he praised him with the utmost enthusiasm. But it was the subsequent line from Heckel, coming just one sentence later, that challenged my view of the world. Still speaking of Bonhoeffer, Pastor Heckel added, "He has in addition the special Pauline advantage in that he is unmarried."[4]

The Pauline *what*?

There I was, reading *Bonhoeffer*, still enchanted by a wiser and much grander "me," only to be confronted by a great private struggle. Like Bonhoeffer before me, I, too, was unmarried. My extended season of singleness—which had lasted for years at this point—felt more like a punishment than a "Pauline advantage." It felt like my life could not, would not, or should not begin until I had a wife at my side. And yet, here I saw another man—a godly man—affirming Paul's words from 1 Corinthians 7. Heckel praised Dietrich Bonhoeffer *because* he was single. He even claimed that this singleness was to his great benefit.

The Pauline advantage of being single.

How could that possibly be?

As I pondered that thought (more thinking about thinking), I considered the words that I

> *He has in addition the special Pauline advantage in that he is unmarried.*
>
> —THEODOR HECKEL

fought with so much. "I say this for your own benefit," Paul said to his readers. Paul genuinely believed that his advice was good. And what benefit did he say that their singleness provided? An undivided devotion to the Lord (1 Corinthians 7:35).

"Are you free from a wife?" he asked. *Do not seek a wife.*

"Are you unmarried or widowed?" *Remain as I am.*

As you might imagine, Paul's words had brought me to a fork in the road. They forced me to wrestle with many unwanted questions. For example, could I call myself a Christian while ignoring Paul's letter? How would my life change if his opinions were true? And then, the most dangerous question of all:

What if our singleness *is* an advantage?

That was the day this book was born. I had made my decision, right then and there, to simply give it a try. I would take Paul at his word. If he was single and Bonhoeffer was single, then perhaps I could follow in their footsteps. No longer would I be consumed with seeking a wife. No. My focus would grow much simpler than that—I simply would focus on Jesus.

What happened next was nothing short of radical. Day by day, I saw my character being changed from the inside out. What once felt like torture had been turned into a blessing. Sure, I still had plenty of sin to deal with, and the occasional bout with loneliness, but I was walking in a noticeably different direction. Instead of walking toward marriage, I was walking toward Jesus. I made a concerted effort to give Him my heart, seeing each part of my life as a way to connect with Him. Nothing was off limits. Everything was His. My heart, soul, mind, and strength were focused on the One that I longed for. Without a wife at my side or kids to take care of, I had plenty of time for this process. And then, it hit me:

I was living the Pauline advantage.

And now, you will be too.

What if our singleness is an advantage?

Over the next thirty days, you will be undergoing that very same journey of transformation. Day by day, you will be inviting Jesus into a specific area of your life, aligning your heart with His word and ways. This deep, experiential knowing of Jesus will unlock purpose and hope for your season of singleness, and it will grant you a joy that only He brings.

The journey is broken down into four distinct sections—Heart, Soul, Mind, and Strength—based on Jesus' words in Mark 12:30. In that portion of Scripture, Jesus says, "And you shall love the Lord your God with all your heart and with all your soul and with all your mind and with all your strength." These next thirty days will follow that structure. Each chapter also includes a challenge to complete. In order for us to experience true transformation, we need to put things into practice. That is why, if possible, I encourage you to read this book with a friend or small group. We are far more likely to push forward with community, and it always feels better to be part of a team. In any given chapter, a daily challenge might ask you and your friends to do some writing, walking, or even eating (yeah, you read that right!), and all with the purpose of growing closer to Jesus.

I am here for you, I am praying for you, and I am excited to watch your heart come alive as you focus on Jesus.

It is time that we do some thinking about thinking.

It is time we become single-minded.

Note: This copy of *Single-Minded* also comes with bonus materials and exclusive content. Please visit www.singlemindedbook.com/resources to download your bonuses today!

HEART

DAY ONE

YOUR GOD

Oh, that men would give thanks to the LORD for His goodness, and
for His wonderful works to the children of men! For He satisfies
the longing soul, and fills the hungry soul with goodness.
—PSALM 107:8–9 NKJV

The date was April 14, 1912. The congregants were gathered in the chapel like any other Sunday. After sharing some pleasantries amongst themselves, Captain E. J. Smith and Reverend Ernest Carter led them in a time of prayer. They quietly bowed their heads in reverence. The chapel swayed to and fro with the shift of the waves. But little did they know, just a few hours later, their prayers would take a different tone. Their pristine chapel, which was warm and welcoming on that Sunday morning, would soon be at the bottom of the Atlantic.[5]

The *Titanic* was deemed an "unsinkable ship." It was seen as the crown jewel of human innovation. But our focus today is not on cruise ships or icebergs. Instead, I share this story with you to highlight some prayers—the prayers of those dying in a shipwreck. One might imagine that when those icy waters first touched their skin, the need of those passengers became perfectly evident. They needed a rescuer. They needed a miracle. And what do humans do when we need a miracle? We instinctively cry out to God. We are never more aware of our need for God than the moments we fall into peril. It's that uneasy feeling when your plane hits some turbulence. Or, it might be an illness in yourself or a loved one. Even the greatest of saints were not immune. The apostle Paul once shared this story in a letter to Corinth:

> For we do not want you to be unaware, brothers, of the afflic-
> tion we experienced in Asia. For we were so utterly burdened
> beyond our strength that we despaired of life itself. Indeed,
> we felt that we had received the sentence of death. But that
> was to make us rely not on ourselves but on God who raises
> the dead. (2 Corinthians 1:8–9)

—

We are never more aware of our need for God than the moments we fall into peril.

—

In these moments of despair, these near-death experiences, we become perfectly aware of our dependence on God. But as we start our thirty-day journey together, my first challenge to you is this: Why not focus on Jesus *before* terror strikes? Why not give Jesus access to *all* parts of you? Whether you're in a positive place and life feels awesome or you feel like you're sinking to the bottom of the ocean, the response and remedy are always the same: The answer is to focus on Jesus.

THE MYSTERY OF GOD

When keeping our focus on Jesus, we must first understand God's progressive revelation. God has chosen to reveal Himself in a very specific way, but that way was a mystery for ages. After the fall of man in the Garden of Eden, there was a dividing line between God and humans. In order to bring mankind back to Himself, God revealed Himself to man in stages. First, there was God's covenant with Abraham (where God promised that a great nation would come from his family). Then, God gave His law to Moses (where God revealed more about His character and ways). Next, God made a promise to the family of David (that a savior of Israel would come from his bloodline). For hundreds of years, that was the full extent of God's revelation. The children of God were forced to look *forward*, hoping in an unknown future about which God had hinted.

But then, Jesus showed up. He turned all of God's whispers into tangible realities. He created a larger nation than Abraham's nation. He delivered a greater law than Moses' law. He was, in fact, the promised Messiah from the house of David. As a result, we Christians do not just look forward today; we also look *backward* to God's answered riddle. Jesus is often referred to in Scripture as the "mystery of God." In the words of the apostle Paul, He is:

> God's mystery, that is, Christ Himself, in whom are hidden all the treasures of wisdom and knowledge . . . For in Him all the fullness of Deity dwells in bodily form. (Colossians 2:2–3, 9 NASB)

It would make sense that God—who is and always will be a spirit (John 4:24, 1 John 4:12)—would seem somewhat mysterious to us physical creatures. We humans can shake a friend's hand or hear a friend's voice, but how can we relate to a God that is spirit? How can the Limitless and Shapeless step into that void? *By appearing on terms that we understand.* In other words, God stepped into the void by becoming a man.

Jesus has always been one with the Father. That is why Jesus could authentically say, "If God were your Father, you would love

11

Me" (John 8:42 NASB), and, "Anyone who has seen me has seen the Father" (John 14:9 NIV). Even still, this expression of God remained a mystery to some. Even though God had provided His ultimate revelation—Himself, in human form—there were still many people who were plagued with doubt. As a result, Jesus would speak in parables in order to confuse them. Many people believe that Jesus taught in parables to make things easier, but that is not what the Bible says. Jesus actually taught in parables to *hide* the truth so that only God's people could unlock His riddles. While His parables did enlighten some, they also confused others. To some, they were gospel; to others, they were madness. Even the disciples were confused about why Jesus used parables. Here is how Matthew recounts that story:

> And the disciples came up and said to Him, "Why do You speak to them in parables?" And Jesus answered them, "To you it has been granted to know the mysteries of the kingdom of heaven, but to them it has not been granted. For whoever has, to him more shall be given, and he will have an abundance; but whoever does not have, even what he has shall be taken away from him. Therefore I speak to them in parables; because while seeing they do not see, and while hearing they do not hear, nor do they understand." (Matthew 13:10–13 NASB)

What were these "mysteries of the kingdom" that Jesus was referring to? Well, chief among them was the fact that Jesus—the lowly carpenter from Nazareth—was actually the long-awaited Savior from the house of David. He was the Riddle of God for which Israel had waited.

God was revealing Himself to those who loved Him, and He was hiding Himself from those who hated Him. Jesus spoke in parables to conceal God's mystery. The parables did not make it easier for the doubters to have faith in Him; they actually did the opposite. Once again, God was keeping the knowledge of Himself a secret. Although many saw Him, they still missed the truth. Although many heard Him, they still put Him to death.

Our Joy in Jesus

We have already established that Jesus is the "mystery" of God. The fullness of God was once hidden from man, but now it is revealed through the life of Jesus. The apostle Paul believed that he—along with the other apostles—had been called to enlighten all people to "the plan of the mystery" (Ephesians 3:9 NASB). The revealed mystery of God was Jesus Christ, and God's plan for that mystery was to unite, restore, and redeem His creation. Thanks to the healing work of Jesus, both the Jews and Gentiles can become one nation. Not only that, but God is unifying His church as a spectacle to His creatures—more specifically, "the rulers and the authorities in the heavenly places" (Ephesians 3:10 NASB). These "rulers" and "authorities" are monikers for angels. That's right. God is uniting His church to bear witness to angels! The good angels (who love God) will be delighted by this, and the demons (who hate God) will be put to shame. The church is God's trophy, lifted high in the heavens. For ages and ages, times and times, the entire universe will know of His victory. As it says in the book of Ephesians:

> But God, being rich in mercy, because of His great love with which He loved us, even when we were dead in our wrongdoings, made us alive together with Christ (by grace you have been saved), and raised us up with Him, and seated us with Him in the heavenly places in Christ Jesus, so that in the ages to come He might show the boundless riches of His grace in kindness toward us in Christ Jesus. (Ephesians 2:4–7 NASB)

Why did God reveal the Mystery? Why did He forgive us and wipe out our debts? So that His grace and mercy could be witnessed forever. For everyone who lives on the new earth with God, we will all know just how we arrived there. It is only because of God's grace and mercy that we'll live in paradise forever.

Jesus is the mystery's conclusion. Jesus is the riddle's answer. In that sense, we immediately arrive when we set out to find Him, knowing that anyone who seeks Jesus inevitably finds Him. But in another sense, we will never understand God completely—not in this life, anyway—because we only see dimly on this side of heaven (1 Corinthians 13:12). And that is why we look to Jesus. He is our endless hope, our unceasing adventure. He is an immediate gift, and our unending prize. He is the spirit of God in the form of a man, thus giving us the ability to trust in Him more. As Louisa M. R. Stead once wrote in her beautiful hymn:

> *Jesus, Jesus, how I trust Him*
> *How I've proved Him o'er and o'er*
> *Jesus, Jesus, precious Jesus*
> *Oh, for grace to trust Him more.*[6]

What we think about God (and Jesus) is crucial. It is the lens through which we see the world. What we think about God, in the deepest respect, will determine what we think about everything else. Is God real? Is He close? Was He truly embodied in Jesus of Nazareth? The Christian can answer a threefold *yes*.

If Jesus is truly your answer, your conclusion, your prize, then let this be your prayer for the next thirty days:

Jesus, Jesus, how I trust You
How I've proved You o'er and o'er
Jesus, Jesus, precious Jesus
Oh, for grace to trust You more.

TODAY'S CHALLENGE

Spend some time in prayer.

Ask God to give you a heightened desire for Jesus. Ask Him to help you grow in your knowledge and trust of Jesus. Ask Him to open your heart over the next thirty days, ensuring that you grasp the full depth of His Mystery.

DAY TWO

YOUR SELF

For whoever desires to save his life will lose it, but
whoever loses his life for My sake will f nd it.
—MATTHEW 16:25 NKJV

I played four years of professional baseball af:er graduating from college. For those four seasons, I did everything I could to realize my dream. But while I certainly wanted to ge: to the Big Leagues, I also knew that the odds were against me. As a result, I always wanted to have a Plan B, which is why I decided to start a business on the side. We sold protein bars. With a natural interest in health and nutrition—plus a college degree in business administration—this seemed like a natural fit for me.

After nearly a year of planning, we officially launched. The company was called "I AM BAR," and our marketing message was simple: You have the power to create your life. I: was all about self-image, self-assurance, self-confidence, and so on. I also couldn't help but smile when I realized that our name—*I AM*—also happened to be the name of God (Exodus 3:14). Eventually, some Christian radio stations caught wind of our products, and they even gave us a few shout-outs on air.

I must admit, between the radio spots and our customer

engagement, it seemed that everything was going to plan. We might have been small, but we were mighty, and we were becoming known as a "Christian" brand. I felt good about that. However, sometimes, what appears on the surface is not true underneath.

What was the slogan of this "God-fearing" business?

Define yourself.

Oh, how the focus groups loved that. If our customers wanted self-empowerment, then self-empowerment is what they would get. We ran marketing campaigns with sayings like "I AM *Healthy*, I AM *Strong*, I AM *Capable*," and so on. But here's the problem: Even those free radio spots and marketing campaigns were not enough. They didn't work. My company failed a few years later. No wonder. I was pushing a message that said we have the power, but the Bible makes it clear that God is our strength. The Bible says that God "opposes the proud" and "gives grace to the humble" (Proverbs 3:34; James 4:6; 1 Peter 5:5). Despite that clear warning, I was encouraging my customers to elevate themselves. But the commands of Scripture say exactly the opposite. As beautifully written by the hand of David:

> The sacrifices of God are a broken spirit, A broken and a contrite heart—These, O God, You will not despise. (Psalm 51:17 NKJV)

I AM *broken*. I AM *contrite*. You will never see that message come out of a focus group! David's words are so countercultural, so perfectly opposed to what our flesh wants, but God's kingdom has always appeared to be backward. The weak are made strong, the last are made first, and it is "losing our life" that allows us to find it. It is only by the complete and utter loss of self—our self-indulgence, our self-importance, our self-esteem, and so on—that life can begin to make sense for us. By forgetting ourselves and focusing on Jesus, we will find the joy that we seek. In the words of C. S. Lewis:

The moment you have a self at all, there is a possibility of putting yourself first—wanting to be the centre—wanting to be God ... And out of that hopeless attempt has come nearly all that we call human history—money, poverty, ambition, war, prostitution, classes, empires, slavery—the long terrible story of man trying to find something other than God which will make him happy.[7]

It is once we finally die to the self that our true nature is actually revealed to us.

When we die to ourselves and receive Christ as our savior, we can take on and delight in the names that God gives to us. Throughout the pages of Scripture, God calls us His sons, His daughters, His friends, His saints, His slaves, His soldiers, His priests, and His bride. We are who God says we are. As single-minded Christians, we choose to become dead to ourselves and alive in our Christ.

As we focus on Jesus, we lose sight of the self. As we focus on Jesus, our self comes alive.

—

The moment you have a self at all, there is a possibility of putting yourself first—wanting to be the centre— wanting to be God.

—C. S. LEWIS

—

Today's Challenge

Answer the following questions:

What is the "self" that your flesh desires? How might this "self" be misaligned with the Scriptures?

_____

_____

_____

_____

What is the "self" that your Savior desires? How can you express this true version of yourself today?

_____

_____

_____

_____

DAY THREE

YOUR FAMILY

Honor your father and your mother, that your days may be
long in the land that the Lord your God is giving you.
—EXODUS 20:12

S ome of the greatest blessings that this world can offer can come
through the love of a family. Even still, some family relationships
can be tough to navigate. Oftentimes, it is actually the members
of our family—the people who are supposed to love us most—who
have the greatest ability to hurt us. Why? Because family relationships
run deeper. The stakes are higher when it comes to family.

How, then, can we grow closer to Jesus by relating to our families?
How can we leverage our bloodlines to strengthen our love, joy, hope,
and holiness, and then bless other people because of it? The Bible gives
two distinct, seemingly opposing commands on how we are to relate
to our families, and the first one we will dive into now.

HONOR

From the beginning to the end of the Bible, from Genesis through
Revelation, God repeatedly tells His children to honor their parents.

It was the fifth commandment that God passed down to Moses (Exodus 20:12), and it is equally relevant today. Quoting that very same command, the apostle Paul wrote this to the church at Ephesus:

> Children, obey your parents in the Lord, for this is right. "Honor your father and mother"—which is the first commandment with a promise—"so that it may go well with you and that you may enjoy long life on the earth." (Ephesians 6:1–3 NIV)

This promise that Paul is alluding to was given to the people of Israel. As they waited to enter the promised land, God literally told them that they would live longer if they honored their parents. By showing them respect and following their teachings, God would add more years to their lives. This was quite a promise for the children of Israel! And yet, Paul used that very same promise to preach to the Ephesians, which means we also should heed it. Like the Old Testament Israelites, like the first-century Ephesians, you and I are called by God to honor our parents.

While this teaching in Scripture is clear and consistent, our society has distanced itself from it. Fewer institutions (and people) than ever before believe that children should be subject to their parents. Some parents would rather be "friends" with their kids than do the hard job of parenting. It is also worth noting that my generation (the Millennials) is predicted to be the first generation in American history to not outlive its parents.[1] That prediction is really quite interesting, especially in light of God's promise to Israel. *If you honor your parents, you will live a long life.* Is it any wonder that as we honor our parents less, we are dying out sooner?

Now, the skeptic in you might object to this thinking. I can understand why. *Come on, Bob, you don't actually believe that honoring our parents can make us live longer, do you? Our declining lifespans in*

America are due to bad diets, poor sleep, chronic stress, and many other factors!

Exactly.

That is exactly my point. While God still reserves the right to be spiritual, perform miracles, and do things that shock and awe us mortals, can His commands not also be perfectly practical? Tell me: What are some of the life lessons that your parents or grandparents taught you as a child? What did they say in the days of your youth?

Eat your vegetables.

Get to bed.

The sun will come out tomorrow.

Perhaps God's command to honor our parents is not entirely spiritual. If we honor our parents and obey their commands, we will typically live longer and happier lives. Why? Because they have been doing this longer than we have. They have seen many more trips around the sun, which means they are wise beyond our years.

But this "honoring" should take us beyond blind obedience. In the book of Leviticus, God also says, "You shall rise before the gray headed and honor the presence of an old man, and fear your God: I am the LORD" (Leviticus 19:32 NKJV). In this example, this "gray headed" man has not issued a command. He has simply walked into the room. As a sign of respect and honor, God wants His children to rise to their feet and revere older people. We are to hold our elders in the highest regard.

As we focus on Jesus more and more, our family should feel increasingly honored. As they enjoy our presence, we enjoy the fruits of reciprocal love. There is, however, another command of Scripture pertaining to family life. It can ruffle some feathers, and it is far less popular, but it is equally important to God.

—

As we focus on Jesus more and more, our family should feel increasingly honored.

—

FORSAKE

When you wholeheartedly devote your life to God, a shift will begin to take place. In some ways, you will experience a deeper connection with family, but in other ways, you might also experience some distancing from them. As you continue to grow in your personal faith, your family might not choose to walk the same path. The fact is, they might not want to grow in their faith. They might actually prefer the status quo, and the changes in you are a threat to their "normal." And that is where the tension begins. Few Christians are prepared for this family separation. And just to be clear, this distancing is not reserved for dysfunctional families. It is literally a command for all of us.

The most obvious example of a command to "forsake" is written in the gospel of Luke. At that point in Jesus' ministry, many large crowds had started to follow Him. They had heard the rumors, they had seen the signs, and they wanted to take part in the spectacle. For that reason, they were ready to follow Him—magnetically drawn to the glitz and glamour. But Jesus had a different message to send. It would not be all fun and games with Jesus. Turning to the starry-eyed crowd who gathered around Him, Jesus said:

> If anyone comes to me and does not hate his own father and mother and wife and children and brothers and sisters, yes, and even his own life, he cannot be my disciple. (Luke 14:26)

Wait. Whoever does not *hate* his father cannot follow Jesus? Whoever does not *hate* his mother is not a true Christian? If you have never heard those words before, then I can imagine that part of you might be offended. In fact, you are probably thinking the same thing as the Jews, staring blankly at Jesus in the Promised Land sun. *Hate my parents?* they must have thought. *That sure doesn't sound very godly to me!*

The first thing worth explaining is Jesus' use of the word "hate."

He is not using the word in a literal sense, like when God says that He *literally* hates divorce (Malachi 2:16), pride (Proverbs 8:13), and a lying tongue (Proverbs 6:16–17). No. Jesus' use of the word "hate" here should read much more like "forsake." Therefore, what Jesus is actually saying is that whoever is not willing to *forsake* their family and put Jesus first is not truly a follower of His. They are, in reality, fake Christians. They are not disciples at all, despite what they say.

But let's not forget, Jesus did not stop at just telling us to "hate" our parents. Notice what He said at the end of that verse. We also must hate *our own lives*. As we discussed in detail yesterday, the self is in direct opposition to God, so Jesus saw fit to add our "self" to His list. Who must we forsake in order to put Jesus first? Ourselves, our parents, our children, our spouses, and anyone else who might pull us from Him.

I understand that these words might be hard to fathom. For your sake, I hope that you have an amazing family, and I hope that your relationships with them are good and strong. If that is the case for you, then the thought of "hating" or "forsaking" them might feel out of bounds. I myself have certainly felt this wrestling.

A few years ago, I felt like the Lord wanted me to move to Nashville. I had no idea why, and I had no clear reason to do so. My life and family were in California, and a cross-country move meant I'd be leaving my loved ones. After a few months of prayer, fasting, and waiting on God, I felt like my moving to Nashville was what God desired. And so, I moved. I packed up my things and drove across the country. Sure, I was excited to step out in faith and follow the Lord, but there was also a significant loss that came with it. Nowadays, I live two thousand miles away from my loved ones. I see them a few times a year on vacations and holidays. Is it enough for my liking? Not even close. Are there times when I question my move to Nashville? More than you know. Will I not be there as my parents grow older? Will I not be around in their moments of need? What happens when I start to have nieces and nephews? Will I miss every Little League game? Every dance recital? Every birthday? Every graduation? Can I really be "Uncle" if I'm never around?

Needless to say, I know the pain of forsaking one's family.

It is only once we are willing to stand firm in our faith that Jesus becomes the center of our lives. Do I believe that you have to move across the country in order to "forsake" your family? No. Am I any "more Christian" because I drove out to Nashville? Absolutely not. I love my family, and they also are Christians. My point here is this: There is no one on earth—not a mother, father, sibling, or spouse— who is more important to us than Jesus. Sometimes, the decision to love Him will cost us greatly, but that does not mean it is wrong.

THE ETERNAL FAMILY

The written Word of God—and the spoken words of Jesus—consistently put forward two commands about families. We are called to both honor and forsake our family. But Jesus also went beyond practicalities, addressing the family in the scope of eternity. As it turns out, God has a different definition of family than we do.

In Matthew 12, we hear a story about Jesus when He was speaking to the crowds. Then, somebody told Him that his mother and brothers were standing outside. They wanted to speak with Him privately, which would have ended His sermon. But Jesus, going very much against the culture of the day, stayed put. He dishonored His family and did not go see them. Instead of appeasing them, He leveraged that moment to deliver a message, forever changing how Christians should relate to their families. In the words of Matthew:

> Jesus replied to the one who was telling Him and said, "Who is My mother, and who are My brothers?" And extending His hand toward His disciples, He said, "Behold: My mother

and My brothers! For whoever does the will of My Father who is in heaven, he is My brother, and sister, and mother." (Matthew 12:48–50 NASB)

It cannot be overstated how offensive this was. Jesus was offending His family—on purpose—in order to prove a point. He was not implying that an earthly family is bad, but rather, that our heavenly family should always take precedence. Who was it that Jesus referred to as brothers? *His disciples.* Who were His sister and mother of choice? *Whoever does the will of God.*

When it comes down to it, the single-minded Christian chooses the things of God over the things of man. According to Jesus, it is not only the blood in our veins that should dictate our family; it is also the God that we worship. Jesus elevates the spiritual family to be on par with the physical family. The good news is, if we love our families in the way that God asks, we will grow closer to Him and to them.

> *It is not only the blood in our veins that should dictate our family; it is also the God that we worship.*

TODAY'S CHALLENGE

Do something special to honor your parents
(or another close family member).

Pick up the phone and call them. Write them a letter. Tell them what you appreciate about them. Say it out loud!

YOUR FRIENDS

The righteous choose their friends carefully, but
the way of the wicked leads them astray.
—PROVERBS 12:26 NIV

Since moving to Nashville at the age of twenty-five, I have healed immensely in the area of friendships. I believe that my season of singleness is responsible for that healing. The truth is, I rarely felt like part of the group when I was growing up. In one way or another, I think most people feel the same way. We are just trying to fit in as best we can, and oftentimes, we feel unsuccessful.

In my story, I was outwardly popular, but I still felt like a bit of an outcast. This feeling started in high school, where I was the captain of sports teams and a good student in class, but I also became known as a "straight edge." I was rarely invited to social engagements. My peers knew that I was uninterested in drinking, smoking, and sleeping around, and thus, the invitations never came. I felt respected, but not known. My name was in the newspaper, but not on the invitation. I felt terribly lonely.

This feeling only increased when I stepped into professional base-ball, where my teammates could be cut or traded with a second's notice. It was not a rare occurrence for me to wake up in the middle of the night, cell phone buzzing, and then have to watch my roommate start packing his bags. Why? Because he had just been traded to the Yankees, the Red Sox, or some other team, and I would likely never see him again. I would arrive at the ballpark later that day and find a new person—a new friend, of sorts—who would be wearing his very same uniform. As a subconscious means of self-protection, I started thinking that I did not need friends. *Friends always leave. Friends are transactional.* That created an ungodly belief about friendships, and one that kept me in bondage for years: *If my friends always leave, then why even try?*

My view of friendship was jaded. My heart had grown cold. I was tired of friendships that felt so transient. They seemed risky and fruitless, and I was tired of extending the offer. My deep desire was to have friends (and keep them), but in a season where I was not pursuing the Lord, I turned to an idol instead. In the absence of companions, I decided that I would simply wait for a wife to become my best friend. *She will stay,* I said to myself. *Surely, she won't leave me like the rest of them have.*

No wonder my heart was in pain.

None of that thinking was biblical.

A LOST ART

—

A friend has the ability to fulfill us in ways that our spouse never could.

—

Our spouse cannot be our only companion. He or she is not going to save us. A friend, however, has the ability to fulfill us in ways that our spouse never could, and this is a truth that we often miss.

In today's society, the romantic relationship is praised above all. We see it in movies, we hear it in songs, and our hearts are quick to take hold of it. Friendship, on the other hand, rarely ever gets its day in the sun. But this distance between friends was not God's design, nor is it the norm throughout history. As C. S. Lewis once observed:

> To the Ancients, Friendship seemed the happiest and most fully human of all loves; the crown of life and the school of virtue. The modern world, in comparison, ignores it.[8]

So, then, why do we in the modern world ignore the blessing of friendship? Why do we banish this "school of virtue"? In my estimation, I think the cause of this dilemma is simple: We glorify marriage and romance too much. The pendulum has swung too far to one side, and friendship has been cast to the shadows. *Friendship is great, but marriage is heaven*—or so says the thinking of the day.

When we miss out on friendships because of this lie, we miss out on the joys that God wants for us. It was my season of singleness that taught me this truth. Day after day, when my wife never came, I was forced to seek out companionship elsewhere. Naturally, a new group of friends soon began to emerge. I was forced to go deeper and deeper with them. And then, something amazing happened. These friends *did* fulfill me. They *did* bring me joy in lieu of a wife. They did not fulfill my every need, but they did fill my cup in their time and way.

As I continued to heal and throw out the old lies, I could finally see the blessing of friendship. It was not lost on me that Jesus once said, "Greater love has no one than this, that someone lay down his life for his friends" (John 15:13). Knowing that Jesus put such an emphasis on the love between friends, I knew that I needed to do the same. A married life *without friends* would not be a complete life either.

The Company We Keep

It is amazing how impressionable we humans can be. We often become like the people we surround ourselves with, which is why it is so important to choose our friends wisely. For me personally, it was not long after my move to Nashville that I noticed my speech had changed. All of a sudden, my g's had disappeared. They vanished. I had been *living* in California for all of my life, but now I was *livin'* in Tennessee. Perhaps you have had a similar experience. It is not rare for someone to come back from a trip to London, Sydney, or some other remote place and notice a change in their accent. And what lesson can we learn from this shift in their speech? Well, to put it plainly, we must choose our friends with the utmost intention because we eventually become more like them. The Bible repeats this point again and again, saying things like:

> Whoever walks with the wise becomes wise, but the companion of fools will suffer harm. (Proverbs 13:20)

> Make no friendship with a man given to anger, nor go with a wrathful man, lest you learn his ways and entangle yourself in a snare. (Proverbs 22:24–25)

> Do not be misled: "Bad company corrupts good character." (1 Corinthians 15:33 NIV)

Bad company corrupts good character. For this reason, it is especially important for us to be around Christians. If we truly want to pursue God with all of our heart, soul, mind, and strength, then we must spend time with people who are doing the same.

We also need friends who can be lovingly honest. They have to be willing to say the hard thing—and even risk offending us—in order to tell us the truth. And when I use the word "offend," I do not mean that they are being malicious or intending to harm; I simply mean that they are willing to say the hard thing. It is the kind of truth that we probably need to hear, but we really don't want to. It is the kind of truth that takes courage and love to share, and the one that only a friend can deliver. In the words of King Solomon:

> Wounds from a friend can be trusted, but an enemy multiplies kisses. (Proverbs 27:6 NIV)

Do you have friends who are able to wound you? Have you given them permission to have a voice in your life, offer you counsel, and say the hard thing when life calls for it? If you were living in sin, would you let them rebuke you? We need friends who are willing to do this for us, and we need to be that friend in return. It is much better to be the friend who tells a hard truth than the enemy who "multiplies kisses."

In our season of singleness, one of the greatest lessons we can learn is the blessing of friendships. A future spouse will not meet every need, and they were never meant to carry the whole load. It took me a while to learn that truth. Nevertheless, the greatest friendship we can ever have is a friendship with our Maker. This is the friendship that our hearts cry out for. This Friend, Jesus, is loving, courageous, and willing to rebuke. He is perfect in character, and we can trust Him completely. It is for these reasons, among others, that we seek out His friendship. It is for these reasons that we can heal from our past.

As Jesus says in the book of John, "No longer do I call you servants, for the servant does not know what his master is doing; but I have called you friends" (John 15:15). Jesus is

—

Wounds from a friend can be trusted, but an enemy multiplies kisses.

—PROVERBS 27:6 NIV

—

the only friend who will never disappoint us. He is the only friend who knows us completely. He is the only friend who will never be traded, cut, and removed from our lives. He is the only friend who can *promise* to stay.

Our life becomes richer when it's filled with good friends.

Our life becomes whole in a friendship with Jesus.

TODAY'S CHALLENGE

Fill in the blank.

Who are 3–5 "good company" people that you need to spend more time with?

Who are 3–5 people in your life who can say the "hard truth" to you?

_____   _____

_____   _____

_____   _____

_____   _____

_____   _____

YOUR CELIBACY

These are the ones who have not defiled themselves with women, for they
are celibate. These are the ones who follow the Lamb wherever He goes.
—REVELATION 14:4 NASB

You might be tempted to think that this chapter is about sex. Not so. That topic will be addressed in detail on Day Twenty-Eight. In theory, all non-married Christians should be walking in celibacy. However, the majority of singles will eventually be married and enjoy sex with their spouse. Despite rising divorce rates and marriages happening later in life, marriage is still very much the norm. But there is a group of people who choose a different path.

Although their numbers are few, there is a select number of Christians—both men and women alike—who will choose to never be married. This choice is made not out of selfishness or a distaste for children, but rather, it is done as an act of the Holy Spirit. It is, quite literally, a gift from God, and I will never forget the first time I met such a person.

MEETING A CELIBATE

I will never forget the day I met him. For the sake of privacy, let's call this man Connor. In Connor's own words, he had made the decision to be celibate at twenty-two years old. Nowadays, some two decades later, he says that decision has brought him nothing but joy.

When I asked Connor if he ever got lonely, he smiled and said to me, "Bob, at least three times a week, I walk into my house and thank God that I live alone. Many people see me, pity me, and try to fix me, but what they don't understand is just how much I love this. Being celibate is the easiest thing in the world for me. I am not sad, I am not lonely, and I did not make this decision in jest. It is truly the best option for me. I am a happier man as a single man. I believe that God has given me the gift of celibacy."

I had never heard anyone talk like that. As I considered his response, I then understood, perhaps for the first time, that God could actually remove our desire to be married. It was not that Connor wanted to be married and continued to fight it, it was that he literally did not have

—

Being celibate is the easiest thing in the world for me. I am not sad, I am not lonely, and I did not make this decision in jest. I believe that God has given me the gift of celibacy.

—CONNOR

—

the desire. There was no childhood trauma to blame, no ugly breakup story. He simply did not get lonely in singleness. He also did not feel a great need for sex. Instead, his life was filled with ministry and friendships. He was simply living a life like Paul's.

I was then faced with the fact that it might be possible—and even biblical—for God to bless someone with the gift of celibacy. In fact, that is exactly how Paul described it in 1 Corinthians 7: *a gift.* He wrote, "I wish that all were as I myself am. But each has his own gift from God, one of one kind and one of another" (1 Corinthians 7:7).

Because Paul did not have a wife or family to care for, that meant that he could pick up and leave at a moment's notice. He could travel an untold number of miles, and face many atrocities, without a second thought. When he was beaten by his captors, there was no wife at home whose heart would be broken. When he was shipwrecked three times, there was no family dinner that he was going to miss. Paul could obey the Lord without hesitation. He was living alone, but walking with God. The very same thing could be said about Connor.

"My default response is always *yes*," Connor continued. "Can you join us on a mission trip to Africa? *Yes*. Can you organize a meal for two hundred church members? *Yes*. Because I am making decisions for just one person, there is rarely anything that stops me from serving. While I still pray about these things and ask the Lord what to do, it is almost always a yes when I'm asked."

"But how can we know if we have such a gift?" I asked. "How can we know if God made us to be celibate?"

"It's hard to say," Connor replied. "I think a good place to start is your desires. Take me, for example. I have absolutely no desire to be married. The thought of it actually exhausts me. For someone like me, being single for a lifetime will be quite easy, while singleness makes most people feel sad. We don't need to overthink this. If you are single and sad, then you probably do not have the gift of celibacy. But if you do not have a desire to seek a spouse, or you do not have a strong urge for sex, then there is nothing wrong with that, either. There is no biblical teaching that requires us to marry."

THE SPIRITUAL GIFT OF CELIBACY

Connor had given me much to ponder. When I turned to Scripture to learn about celibacy, there was one key teaching from the mouth of Jesus. Truth be told, I had glossed over it every time I read it in the past, but a conversation with Connor had opened my eyes. Speaking to His disciples, Jesus said this:

> For there are eunuchs who have been so from birth, and there are eunuchs who have been made eunuchs by men, and there are eunuchs who have made themselves eunuchs for the sake of the kingdom of heaven. Let the one who is able to receive this receive it. (Matthew 19:12)

A eunuch (pronounced *yoo-nek*) is someone who is either incapable of, or unwilling to, engage in sexual activity. In biblical times, male slaves were oftentimes "made eunuchs by men" when they were forcibly castrated by their masters, thus preventing these slaves from sleeping with their master's wife or daughter. But Jesus presented two other types of eunuchs. There are also eunuchs who have been born that way (without sexual desires), and others who have chosen that life in order to serve God. (I was starting to see images of Connor and Paul.) I also found it interesting that even the book of Revelation—speaking of life in the new heavens and new earth—makes a specific reference to eunuchs and celibacy. Describing his vision of the end times, the apostle John wrote:

> And they sang a new song before the throne and before the four living creatures and the elders; and no one was able to learn the song except the 144,000 who had been purchased from the earth. These are the ones who have not defiled themselves with women, for they are celibate. These are the ones who follow the Lamb wherever He goes. (Revelation 14:3–4 NASB)

Isn't that interesting? What a peculiar detail for John to include. But then again, what a blessed gift that these celibates have! *They follow the Lamb wherever He goes.* Much like the apostle Paul, a celibate single is always ready for deployment. They can go wherever they are needed. They can heal, restore, and rejuvenate. If a need arises, their default is *yes*. Like a red blood cell in the body of Christ, a celibate single is uniquely designed to serve the church.

Needless to say, I left my conversation with Connor with a new take on marriage. There was another path—celibacy—that I had never considered before. The Pauline advantage was once again surfacing.

A Tale of Two Horses

There is a famous parable in small business circles. Perhaps you have heard it. I call this parable the "tale of two horses." It has become a staple for sales and motivation, and it is often used as a lesson on teamwork. The story goes something like this:

A farmer takes his horse to the fair. That horse proceeds to set a record for the largest weight towed—*eight thousand pounds!* But then, that farmer takes his horse and yokes it to another, wanting to see how much two horses can tow. (Perhaps you can see where this story is going.) Much to the people's dismay, the pair of horses tow not just two times as much, but *three* times as much. Through the power of teamwork, they can now tow a whopping twenty-four thousand pounds. By deciding to work as a team, the first horse can now tow three times as much as he could on his own.

At this point, you can probably see why a leader might like this story. Its moral is simple: We are greater than the sum of our parts. However, this lesson is actually wrong in some situations. This metaphor does not hold true for all seasons of life. In the case of Paul, Connor, and perhaps even you, this lesson does not fit in the case of the celibate.

For the sake of example, let's imagine a sequel to the tale of two horses. Let's imagine that those same two horses, teamwork and all, went to a racetrack instead of the fair. They are faced with a brand-new dilemma—instead of hauling weight, they are running a race. Tell me, would yoking these horses together make them run any faster? Of course not. In fact, it would do the exact opposite! The slower of the two horses would slow down the faster horse, every time, guaranteed. When it comes down to it, being yoked to a partner actually hurts you in sprinting.

So then, let me ask you: Should horses be yoked together or not? Should we tie horses together if we enter a contest? What once seemed obvious now requires some thinking. The reality is our answer will always depend on the task. Some horses need a partner in order to tow. Some horses need freedom in order to run. The task of the horse will determine the need.

And it is exactly the same with relationships.

Some horses need a partner in order to tow. Some horses need freedom in order to run.

While very few people are like Paul or Connor, it is important for us to consider their gift. If you are holding this book in your hands, then you likely find yourself in a season of singleness. Have you pondered if God has equipped you for celibacy? Have you ever considered that you might have this gift?

Even if you do not possess the gift of celibacy, just asking these questions is a valuable exercise. If you wholeheartedly devote your life to God, then that means that everything—even your right to marriage—has to be fully surrendered to Him. You might very well be married one day, and if that is the Lord's plan for you, then you can trust that your marriage will eventually come. You are, however, still called to a wholehearted, single-minded devotion to God today.

Marriage is just one fork in the road.

The road less traveled is celibacy.

TODAY'S CHALLENGE

Spend some time in prayer.

Consider the possibility of being single forever. Ask God to guide you on the path that He wants for you, and ask Him to bring your desires in alignment with His. This might be a difficult exercise for you (all acts of surrender are!), but the end goal is to draw your heart closer to God. By the end of your prayer time, you should feel closer to, and more trusting in, the God who created you and loves you deeply.

YOUR DATING

Promise me, O women of Jerusalem, not to awaken love until the time is right.
—SONG OF SOLOMON 8:4 NLT

Biblically speaking, there are just two major relationship statuses. You are single, or you are married. The time in between these two statuses—whether we call it dating, engagement, or betrothal—should be naturally short and intentional. But just to be clear, my goal for this chapter is not to prescribe a formula. This is not meant to provide you with "biblical dating" in three easy steps. My goal for this chapter—and for this entire book—is simply to remind you of where our focus should be. The message and mantra is always the same: *Focus on Jesus, no matter the season.* Therefore, if we possess a single-minded, wholehearted devotion to Christ, then how should we approach the topic of dating? What verses in the Bible would support our beliefs? How might we date in our culture today? That is what today's chapter is about.

Paul's Binary Teaching

In light of Paul's words on marriage in 1 Corinthians 7, the single-minded Christian chooses one of two options: He either chooses to be married—and gets married quickly (1 Corinthians 7:9)—or he chooses to be single and "remain as he is" (1 Corinthians 7:26). Paul does not leave us much room for alternative options. He says that our natural desires will show us the way. Notice what Paul says to the Christians at Corinth:

> To the unmarried and the widows I say that it is good for them to remain single, as I am. But if they cannot exercise self-control, they should marry. For it is better to marry than to burn with passion. (1 Corinthians 7:8–9)

Paul's teaching was simple: If you can, stay single; if you can't, get married. Are you burning with sexual or relational passion? Then find yourself a partner and get married now. This is truly an if/then statement in Paul's eyes. If you are burning with passion, then it's best you get married. Of course, we want to entrust these decisions to the will of the Lord, but Paul's words provide a general principle.

As we discussed in the last chapter, the Christian's default is always celibacy, even if that path is later abandoned. Paul further affirms this fact in his letter to the Corinthians, speaking of the man who has tamed his desires:

> But the man who has settled the matter in his own mind, who is under no compulsion but has control over his own will, and who has made up his mind not to marry the virgin—this man also does the right thing. So then, he who marries the virgin does right, but he who does not marry her does better. (1 Corinthians 7:37–38 NIV)

The God-focused heart begins with celibacy. It focuses on the things of the Lord. It grows in holiness and maturity, and it finds hope and joy in its Maker. But then, if the passions of the flesh refuse to be stifled, we acknowledge that fact, and we step into marriage.

Now, just to be clear, I understand that spouses do not grow on trees. Simply saying, "I am burning with passion! I want to be married!" does not mean it will happen tomorrow. I personally have experienced great frustration in this. Despite my efforts to find a wife, despite going on dates, despite being set up by strangers at church, marriage has yet to become a part of my story. It is still a great desire of mine, but it is a desire that has gone unmet. Perhaps you've experienced a similar path. Sometimes, it is just not our turn to step into marriage. The waiting in between, however—and the pain and frustration it oftentimes brings—does not permit us to date unintentionally. Did you notice what Paul did not mention in his letter?

Dating for the sake of it. Dating for fun.

Paul's equation for relationships is perfectly binary. *If you can, stay single; if you can't, get married.* Therefore, if we have not been given the gift of celibacy, then our path of obedience is marriage, not dating—and that is an important distinction. The goal is marriage. Dating without a goal is not at all biblical. (I'm not talking about high school kids who are going to the prom. I am talking about casual dating between two adults.)

When our goal for dating is anything but marriage, we might be involved in a practice quite sinister. If we aren't considering this person as a possible mate, then what, I ask, are we doing? Are we not just seeking a bandage, a mask, or a drug of some kind? Are we not choosing short-term comforts over long-term commitments? When it comes down to it, we are stealing.

Sometimes, it is just not our turn to step into marriage. The waiting in between, however—and the pain and frustration it oftentimes brings— does not permit us to date unintentionally.

The Timing of Love

In 1 Corinthians 7, Paul tells us to focus on heavenly things. He knew how a romance could capture the mind. "Are you free from a wife? Do not seek a wife," he says. Paul feels this way not because he hates romance or despises relationships, but rather because he had seen earthly marriages distance people from God. We will discuss the value and holiness of marriage tomorrow, but for now, we will focus on the advantage of singleness. The apostle Paul writes:

> I want you to be free from anxieties. The unmarried man is anxious about the things of the Lord, how to please the Lord. But the married man is anxious about worldly things, how to please his wife, and his interests are divided. (1 Corinthians 7:32–34)

The truth is, we spend a lot of time with the person we are dating. When in the early stages of dating, we are swept up by passion and feelings of joy. This is when poems and notes and love songs are written. But there are risks and challenges in dating as well, because our concerns are now multiplied by two. We have less time for ourselves and the things of the Lord, because some of our focus has been shifted to another. This is what Paul was warning about. When our interests are "divided," we have less time in the day to serve the church, discover our passions, develop our skills, advance professionally, or wait on the Lord to reveal His will. Also—and it might sound strange to say this— we rob ourselves of suffering when we start dating too soon. Make no mistake, it is *suffering*, not pleasure, that develops our character. Hebrews 2:10 says that even Jesus Himself was made perfect through suffering. Now, while some may joke that marriage brings suffering, that is likely not the suffering that you are currently facing. Instead, your suffering is likely one of isolation. You feel unseen, unheard, and unknown by the world. It is this state of loneliness—which is a very real feeling that we should not belittle—that causes many Christians to date prematurely. They look for a human to meet their needs. Sometimes, they actually "succeed" and find a spouse quickly, but this oftentimes comes with a cost. They miss out on suffering that could have been to their benefit.

You feel unseen, unheard, and unknown by the world. It is this state of loneliness that causes many Christians to date prematurely.

But the single person is under no such constraints. The single Christian's time is available for God and for others. We are agile, mobile, and ready to serve. Our lives look a lot like Connor's—my friend whom you met in the last chapter.

I can personally attest to the value of this freedom. My first book, *Our Hearts' Desire*, took about two years for me to complete. That project consumed most of my nonworking time. On most Friday nights, I was reading my Bible. Instead of scheduling dates, I was pondering God. I wrote for roughly two hours a day, every day, for two years. If I'm being honest, I just wasn't that good when I first started out. I needed the time to write, and fail, and write some more. Needless to say, that would not have been possible if I had been in love. God made me an author in that season of life. In the midst of my pain, He brought me my passion. He developed my skill in lieu of a spouse.

He can do the same for you, if you let Him.

FINAL THOUGHTS

I have one last thing to address about dating. I have heard it said—and perhaps you have as well—that God will not bring you a spouse until you no longer want one. "It will happen when you least expect it," they say. "It will happen when you no longer look for it." While there might be some truth to this adage, there is another side to this teaching that I cannot support. This line of thinking puts a remarkable amount of pressure and blame on the unmarried person. *Oh, so God hasn't brought you a spouse yet? Then clearly, you must want it too much!* This statement cannot be true in all situations. It is an exaggeration, it is irresponsible, and it puts the speaker in the place of God. How can we know if they "want it" too much? Alternatively, perhaps God is more concerned with other parts of their life. Perhaps they, like Moses or Joseph or Esther, are in the midst of a God-given trial that will make sense over time. Who are we to provide a diagnosis?

Instead of longing for marriage, coming up empty, and then focusing on Jesus as a consolation prize, why not focus on Jesus from the very beginning, and pursue marriage when the path becomes clear? Marriage is a blessing, yes, but so is God's timing, and God's timing is something worth waiting on.

Biblical dating occurs when we understand marriage.

Biblical dating occurs when we focus on Jesus.

TODAY'S CHALLENGE

If you are currently dating someone—or hope to be dating someone in the near future—review the following questions when considering a marriage partner:

- Is knowing and pursuing Jesus the primary focus of this person's life?
- Do they seek the glory of God and desire to make Him known?
- Is there a "friendship" love between you? Would you enjoy them as a friend if there was not a romance?
- Do they show a consistent pattern of caring about you, your needs, your thoughts, and so on?
- Are the fruits of the spirit (e.g., love, joy, peace, patience, kindness, goodness, faithfulness, gentleness, self-control) evident in their daily life?
- Do you like who you are around them? Do they make you a better person?
- Are they willing and able to forgive?
- Are your dreams, talents, and passions compatible with theirs?
- Have you prayed and asked God to reveal His will for your relationship? (If God said no, would you be willing to walk away?)
- Are your friends and mentors on board with this person? What do they think about them?
- In John 15:13, Jesus says, "Greater love has no one than this, that someone lay down his life for his friends" (NIV). Would you lay your life down for this person?

YOUR MARRIAGE

*For this reason a man will leave his father and mother and be united to
his wife, and the two will become one flesh. This is a profound mystery.*
—EPHESIANS 5:31–32 NIV

Marriage was the very first human relationship. It was not a
friendship, not a relationship between siblings, coworkers,
or friendly neighbors—it was a marriage with which God
began our race. Marriage is the most intimate of human relationships,
because a marriage most closely reflects God's oneness. Let's spend a
few minutes discussing our marriages.

FULFILLING YOUR SPOUSE

In all of the marriage books that I have read, I have not found a single title—not one—that covers what I am about to share with you.
That seems quite peculiar to me, because this teaching of Scripture
can pack quite a punch. It is a short little verse, tucked away in the
deepest recesses of the Old Testament, but it brings with it a powerful
message. This verse is found in the book of Deuteronomy, and it was

once a command for God's people. From the mouth of God to the pen of Moses, God made this demand of the Israelites:

> A newly married man must not be drafted into the army or be given any other official responsibilities. He must be free to spend one year at home, bringing happiness to the wife he has married. (Deuteronomy 24:5 NLT)

After a miraculous deliverance from Egypt, God proceeded to spend forty years molding, shaping, and refining His people. He wanted to use the nation of Israel as a mouthpiece, a symbol, that would bear His name. Through an extensive series of laws—some of which seemed completely obscure to the outside nations—God revealed His nature to the world. It was the Israelites' job, quite literally, to reveal who God was by obeying His statutes. He wanted this nation of rescues to be viewed as different. Why? Because God is different. God is holy, and the world is not. Therefore, His children would also be holy.

Now, just to be clear, the command of Deuteronomy 24:5 is not binding on us today. You and I live under a completely different covenant, where many Old Testament commandments are no longer applicable. Even still, this verse provides incredible insight into God's feelings on marriage. Here we have God—the Creator of the universe—literally commanding a year-long honeymoon. For their first year of marriage, these newlywed husbands were not responsible for serving in the military or conducting any business—they were simply responsible for pleasing their wives. For an entire trip around the sun, they were called to nurture their marriages.

What hope that can bring if you want to be married! We worship a God who cherishes marriages. Here in America, our newlyweds get excited about one-week honeymoons, flying off to the tropics for snorkeling and rest. But then, seven days later, it is all over. They are back at their desks, back to reality, caught up once again by the hustle and bustle. Their marriages often will take a back seat. But God had a different idea for Israel. Their honeymoons would last an entire year! Can you imagine what that year must have been like for them? Can you imagine the joy and life and love that was shared? It is often said that the best way to spell love is not *L-O-V-E*, but *T-I-M-E*, and God was giving them permission to take it.

For their first year of marriage, these husbands were not responsible for serving in the military or conducting any business—they were simply responsible for pleasing their wives.

There are two lessons to be gleaned from this verse in Deuteronomy. First, God genuinely wants us to enjoy our marriages. If you do end up getting married one day (Lord willing), He will want your marriage to be awesome and life-giving. And secondly, this verse also teaches us that it is in God's nature to prioritize relationships. God wanted Israelite men to devote intentional time to pleasing their spouses. What was His command? *Make your wife happy.*

My point is not that we should plan a 365-day honeymoon. My point is simply that it is in God's nature to nurture a marriage. God invented marriage, He authentically loves it, and He wants our marriages to thrive. He wants them to be happy, healthy, and, dare I say, heavenly. God uses our marriages to reflect Himself. For all of eternity, the Father, Son, and Holy Spirit have been loving, nurturing, and engaging one another. They have been blessing each other with *T-I-M-E*. As God's image bearers, we are meant to treat our spouses in the very same way. It is for this reason that God handed down such an interesting—and hope-inspiring—command in Deuteronomy 24:5.

But there is yet another side of the coin.

Forsaking Your Spouse

The Bible's centerpiece on marriage is Ephesians 5. You will hear this passage read at nearly all Christian weddings, and it will certainly be mentioned in most books on the subject. Its message is simple, yet profound: Wives are supposed to submit to their husbands, as to the Lord (Ephesians 5:22), and husbands are supposed to love their wives sacrificially, as Christ loved the church (Ephesians 5:25). The wife follows, and the husband serves—that is the will of God.

In this hallmark passage of Scripture, Paul is unmistakably fighting for the sanctity of marriages. He literally compares them to the love of the Lord. It might then surprise you to read 1 Corinthians 7, where this very same apostle Paul—the one who encouraged the Ephesians to nurture their marriages—takes a strikingly different tone. Here is what Paul wrote in his letter to Corinth:

> Those who marry will have worldly troubles, and I would spare you that. This is what I mean, brothers: the appointed time has grown very short. From now on, let those who have wives live as though they had none . . . For the present form of this world is passing away. (1 Corinthians 7:28–29, 31)

Let those who have wives live as though they had none? Would Christ ever treat His church in that way? That seems radically different from Ephesians 5!

But that's just it. That is exactly the point.

While Paul's analogy in Ephesians 5 is still perfectly valid, that analogy—like any other description or metaphor about God—cannot fully capture the truth of the matter. Yes, a husband is supposed to love like Christ, and a wife is supposed to submit like the church, but no earthly marriage can fulfill that call perfectly. Much like a mirror's reflection, we humans are only a shade, an image, a reflection, of the actual thing that is Christ's love. Christ and His church are the ultimate marriage, and the object that we seek to reflect.

Now, just as a point of clarity, here is what Paul is *not* saying in 1 Corinthians 7. He is not saying, "Hey, husbands, the present world is passing away. Jesus is coming back soon, so if you have a wife, don't pay her any mind. Feel free to eat, drink, and be merry, and if you find another woman, have fun!"

Not so.

What Paul is saying is simply this: Because we have no idea when Jesus is coming back, we should live our lives as if His return is imminent. We should have our priorities in order, according to the will of God.

So then, tell me this: Is it more important for us to please our spouses or to please the Lord? In the scope of eternity, the answer should be quite obvious. If we care about our eternal resting place, if we care about what happens beyond this life, then God must be our number one focus. When we give our marriages, our spouses, our children, our professions, or anything else the top rung on the ladder, we are doomed to a life of disappointment—in both this world and the next.

The very worst way to love your spouse is to love them more than God. That throne is not meant for them, and the crown is too heavy for them to bear. It is for this reason that we must "forsake" our spouses in order to love them. It is by putting our spouse second, much lower than God, that our marriages will properly function. They are an outward expression of an inward reality. It was Jesus Himself who said, "If anyone comes to me and does not hate his own father and mother and wife and children and brothers and sisters, yes, and even his own life, he cannot be my disciple" (Luke 14:26).

> *The very worst way to love your spouse is to love them more than God.*

Jesus delivered the very same message that Paul would years later: If you find yourself in a Christian marriage, you must "live as if you had none." Jesus was not telling the Israelites to abandon their spouses, nor was He telling them to wish evil upon them. Jesus was simply reminding them that God must come first. That is the recipe for heavenly marriage: God comes first, our spouses second, ourselves a distant third.

FINAL THOUGHTS

There is obvious tension between these two commandments. Both Deuteronomy 24 and Ephesians 5 say that marriage is important, and it should be valued and cared for. But then, 1 Corinthians 7 says that marriage is not the ultimate goal, nor will it provide our ultimate delight. It is the tension between these passages—this theological tug of war—that allows our marriages to reflect God's character. We must remember both sides of the coin: *fulfill* and *forsake*. We are supposed to bring joy to our spouse, and we are called to forsake our spouse. We can focus on marriage, and our marriage can thrive, but not if we make it our idol. Here are the priorities in a heavenly marriage:

God comes first, our spouses second, ourselves a distant third.

TODAY'S CHALLENGE

Schedule a phone call or meal with a married couple you respect. Look for a couple that is considerably older than you, with much greater life experience. Ask them to share their insights and wisdom on the subject of marriage.

Here are some sample questions to get things started:

- What do you wish you knew when you were single?
- What do you wish you had done differently when you were single?
- What have you learned since getting married?
- How have you learned to fulfill your spouse?
- How have you learned to forsake your spouse?

YOUR CHURCH

Then the churches throughout all Judea, Galilee, and Samaria
had peace and were edified. And walking in the fear of the Lord
and in the comfort of the Holy Spirit, they were multiplied.
—ACTS 9:31 NKJV

The crowds had been gathering since earlier that morning. They anxiously awaited the spectacle to come. It was June 30, 1859, and everyone in attendance was expecting a miracle—or the death of a madman.[9]

The man of the hour was Charles Blondin. Hailing from France, Blondin was the most famous tightrope walker in the world. He stood at just five feet, five inches tall, and he had been tightrope walking from the time he was a toddler. His task that day, though obviously quite daring, was simple: He would tightrope across Niagara Falls.

This was an audacious feat for any tightroper. It had never been attempted—let alone completed—but Blondin felt up to the challenge. He laid a rope across the falls, running 1,300 feet in length and just two inches in diameter. For nearly a quarter of a mile, that would be the margin between Blondin and death. Two inches.

Starting on the American side, Blondin set out on his journey to Canada. He walked slowly across the woven cords. But then, at the midpoint of his crossing, Blondin did something that no one expected: he actually sat down on the rope! From his private perch above the waters, he called out to the boat below. The 25,000 people on shore could not make out his words, perhaps thinking that Blondin was calling for help. But the Frenchman was calling for something else. Instead of sending a distress signal, Blondin was seen lowering a rope to the boat. The rope started out empty, but it returned with a gift—a bottle of his favorite wine. He had worked up a thirst after all of his travels.

After taking a swig of the wine, Blondin stood back up, ditched the bottle, and sprinted the rest of the way. He made it to land in the blink of an eye. The onlookers were amazed. How could any man maintain such balance?

Blondin had made history. By daring to do something that no one else dreamed of, he cemented his place as the greatest tightrope walker of all time. He had traveled light on this perilous journey, taking nothing besides what he deemed essential: his pink tights, his thin leather shoes, a camera to snap a few photos, and...

His twenty-six-foot balancing pole.

That pole was what made it all possible.

A BALANCING ACT

Of all the verses in Scripture, perhaps no verse has impacted me more than Acts 9:31. In my experience, I have found that very few people have committed it to memory. I have yet to see Acts 9:31 stitched into a pillow. Even still, this verse provides a clear prescription for growing with God, and, by extension, how our churches can grow as a whole.

The book of Acts describes the history of the first church. Its main actors—people like Peter, Paul, Barnabas, and others—are carrying out the great commission. Jesus had told them to make disciples, baptize, and teach others to obey God's commandments. They went out with boldness and preached the gospel. They walked freely in Jerusalem, debating the Jews, explaining how the Old Testament Scriptures revealed Jesus as Messiah. And then, as Luke wrote in the book of Acts, "Walking in the fear of the Lord and in the comfort of the Holy Spirit, they were multiplied" (Acts 9:31 NKJV).

> —
>
> *We need two distinct things on the tightrope of faith: the fear of the Lord and the comfort of the Holy Spirit.*
>
> —

And therein lies our balancing pole. The single-minded Christian—and the modern-day church as a whole—will only see growth by keeping this balance. True faith needs *balance*. We need two distinct things on the tightrope of faith: the fear of the Lord and the comfort of the Holy Spirit. Let's talk about both, in turn.

The Fear of the Lord

When walking the tightrope of faith, the fear of the Lord is almost always the least popular. Many people assume that by "fearing" the Lord, they are signing up for a lifetime of restrictions, losing their joy, and perpetually getting the short end of the stick. But this could not be further from the truth. By misunderstanding the meaning of fear, we are actually robbing ourselves of comfort. We must remember it was *because* of their fear, not in spite of it, that the church of Acts was multiplied.

Many Christians today—and even some pastors—try to dampen their definitions of fear. They try to make it mean something less than terror or fright, often landing on words like "reverence" and "respect." But this weakening of the word was not God's intention, and it ultimately has a negative effect. The fact is, God is not some "heavenly mayor" that "deserves our respect." He is the Creator of the universe and the Judge of all sin. He has the power—and the right—to literally damn us to hell. That is where true fear comes in. Just as an earthly father can threaten a "spanking" to his children, God also presents a threat of His own. This is why the writers of the Bible use the word "tremble" so often when describing their fear of the Lord. They are not merely expressing a love, affection, or commitment to God; they are expressing a genuine fright. As the psalmist once wrote, "My flesh trembles for fear of You, and I am afraid of Your judgments" (Psalm 119:120 NKJV). In fact, it was Jesus Himself who warned:

> Now I say to you, My friends, do not be afraid of those who kill the body, and after that have nothing more that they can do. But I will warn you whom to fear: fear the One who, after He has killed someone, has the power to throw that person into hell; yes, I tell you, fear Him! (Luke 12:4–5 NASB)

Jesus' teaching on fear takes us well beyond reverence. The hypothetical "murderers" in His example would have struck a sense of terror, a genuine fear, into the hearts of the people who listened. Would you not be alarmed when faced with a killer? Much in the same way, Jesus wants us to fear someone else, someone greater, who can put us in much greater torment. The reason we are to fear the Lord is not just because of His majesty, His gifts, or the brilliance of His creation. No. Our motivation for fear is much simpler than that: We also fear God out of fear of damnation.

According to Jesus, a genuine fear of hell can lead a Christian to holiness. While our God is certainly a loving Father, and Jesus is still our Savior and Friend, there is another side of His nature that is genuinely terrifying. God is also the righteous Judge with the keys to hell, and He lives in unapproachable light (1 Timothy 6:16). But while you might assume that this fear should cause us to run, it will actually have the opposite effect. It is only by contrasting what we should be given (the fires of hell) with what we actually receive (the mercies of God) that the comfort of the Spirit can grip us. It is this truth, this comfort, that causes us to run to our Father.

THE COMFORT OF THE HOLY SPIRIT

In order for comfort to be provided, there must be a need to be met. There must be a pain that is absolved. That is why Christians are in such desperate need of God's comfort today, because we currently live in a fallen world. Our sin-filled planet presents us with many things that were never part of God's design: things like death, disease, heartbreak, betrayal—the list goes on and on. How, then, can we navigate a world filled with so much peril? How can we press on when our strength gives out? *God's comfort.* The comfort of the Holy Spirit.

By understanding the truths of Scripture, a trust in God will permeate your life. Yes, our world is broken, but God still has a plan in motion. He is going to restore this world to its original state—when the fullness of time has been completed—and He is able to protect us in the interim. That is how King David could say, "Even though I walk through the valley of the shadow of death, I will fear no evil, for you are with me; your rod and your staff, they comfort me" (Psalm 23:4). David was comforted because God was with him. It did not matter if he faced evil, danger, or the pains of this world. David knew that God was good. David knew that God was for him.

What incredible strength this truth can bring! No matter what this world throws your way, you have a Lord in Jesus who cares about

It is only by contrasting what we should be given (the fires of hell) with what we actually receive (the mercies of God) that the comfort of the Spirit can grip us.

the outcomes. He cares about your heart's well-being. But we must also remember that Jesus does not promise to fix everything, immediately, just because of our prayers. What He does promise is that He will fix everything, eventually, when this world is redeemed. That is where our comfort comes from. It was Jesus Himself who said, "I have told you these things, so that in me you may have peace. In this world you will have trouble. But take heart! I have overcome the world" (John 16:33 NIV).

Acts 9:31 tells us that there were two specific things that multiplied the church: They had a healthy fear of God and an abounding comfort because of God's promises. A healthy church—and a healthy Christian—will always have a balance of both.

WHEN THINGS GET OFF-BALANCE

Just as Charles Blondin needed both sides of his balancing pole, the church needs both the fear of the Lord and the comfort of the Spirit. We, like the church of Acts 9:31, need balance if we wish to multiply. But sometimes, our personal preferences can get us off track, which can cause deviations from Scripture. We are guilty of leaning to both sides of the rope.

On the "fear of the Lord" side of things, I have personally spoken to estranged Christians—many of whom grew up in a conservative church—who walked away from the faith once they took off for college. At their core, their stories are almost always the same. To these defecting Christians, the church had come to be known as a place of rights, rules, and regulations—and very few smiles. They felt more comfort in *leaving* the church than they did while attending one. In some instances, they had struggled with drug abuse, gotten pregnant out of wedlock, or did something else "shameful" in the eyes of their church. In so many stories of now-*former* Christians, there was a notable lack of comfort provided. When delivering a hard truth, it is often the delivery, not the truth itself, that determines success or failure. When a fear-mongering church does not offer comfort, it is grossly misaligned with God's ways.

On the other side of the coin, a church that leans toward comfort and emotion is much more attractive to sinners. (These are the modern-day churches with lasers and fog machines.) But when things get out of balance—when we prioritize fun and freedom over obeying God's commandments—the results can be quite catastrophic. A common example of this might be found at a concert, where the artist on stage professes to be a Christian. This hip-hop or country artist is excited to express their experience of God, so they attempt to share their version of the gospel. Shouting into the microphone, they say, "God loves you so much! You are beautiful, you are loved, you are important, and don't let anyone tell you any different!" The crowd roars. It scratches the itch. But then, once their spiritual rant is over, the message does not bring transformation. It does not actually change the hearts of the audience. Why? Because that is *not* the gospel message. The Bible does not say that we are awesome, beautiful, and in no need of Jesus. It actually says the opposite—that we are sinful, hell-bound, and in need of a savior. The problem is, the unknowing attendee who has not read the Bible might take these musicians at their word. They might mistakenly believe that they don't have to change, that they don't have to repent, and that they can keep on living their life as they please. There is no fear, no wrath, and no call to repentance that is shared from the stage at these concerts. This is yet another way we can get out of balance, because half-truths can be just as destructive.

When delivering a hard truth, it is often the delivery, not the truth itself, that determines success or failure.

FINAL THOUGHTS

It is for these reasons that we must maintain balance in our churches. We need a fear of the Lord to keep us in line, and we need the comfort of the Spirit to keep us encouraged. Offering more of one and less of the other is not something to be taken lightly.

For the single-minded Christian—just like Charles Blondin—our pathway to success is narrow. Jesus Himself once said, "The path is narrow that leads to life" (Matthew 7:14 NASB95). The path for Blondin was just two inches wide, and there is no telling how narrow ours is. But if there is anything I know, I can guarantee this:

You'll fare better with a balancing pole.

TODAY'S CHALLENGE

Grade yourself, on a scale of 1–10,
on both sides of the pole of faith.

How much fear of the Lord do you live with? How much
comfort of the Holy Spirit do you live with? Circle those
two marks on the pole to get a visual representation of where
you lean.

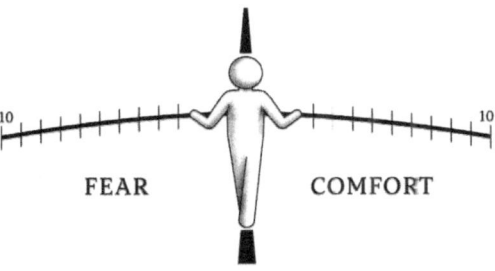

What is one thing you can do to increase your fear of the Lord?

_____

_____

_____

What is one thing you can do to experience more comfort
of the Holy Spirit?

_____

_____

_____

YOUR WORLD

The world cannot hate you, but it hates Me,
because I testify that its works are evil.
—JOHN 7:7 BSB

I only had fourteen minutes to make my flight. Fortunately for me, this was only a short layover on a business trip, which meant that I had fit all my things in a carry-on bag. Nevertheless, I was still worried. My first flight had to circle the airport due to fog, so I was cutting it close on making my connection.

When the plane's wheels finally touched down, we taxied to the gate, and my race was on. If you have ever been to Denver International Airport, you can probably guess what this scene might have looked like. As I frantically sprinted to gate B48, I navigated through a barrage of people, trams, and moving walkways. With the oxygen levels as they are in Denver, I was quickly gasping for air. Sweat cascaded down my brow. It was not a pretty sight! But then, to my pleasant surprise, I made it to my gate on time. Barely. I had discovered the one benefit of Boarding Group 7.

As I caught my breath and waited to board, I started to take note of my surroundings. Looking up at the ceiling, I noticed a large poster that covered the concourse. It boasted a black-and-white photo of Abraham Lincoln, with a sentence imposed across his chest:

> A house divided against itself cannot stand.
> —Abraham Lincoln

Perhaps you have seen this quotation before. It is one of the most famous sayings attributed to Lincoln. But while this poster's message was uplifting and challenging, I couldn't help but notice its obvious error:

That quote is not Abraham Lincoln's.

THE GODLESS GOD

In the third chapter of Mark, the Pharisees are terribly angry with Jesus. He was healing the sick and causing a scene, and He also was casting out demons. The scribes and Pharisees then accused Jesus of wrongdoing, saying, "By the prince of demons he is driving out demons" (Mark 3:22 NIV). This statement puzzled Jesus, as it would any logical mind. Catching these religious elites in their logical fallacy, Jesus asked them rhetorically, "How can Satan drive out Satan?" (Mark 3:23 NIV). He did not wait for an answer. Satan obviously would not drive out Satan. And then, Jesus made a statement that many Christians would use—including Abraham Lincoln, some 1,800 years later—as a reference in their teachings on unity. It was Jesus who originally said:

> If a house is divided against itself, that house cannot stand.
> (Mark 3:25 NIV)

As I looked up at that poster of Abraham Lincoln, I wondered how many people would see it that day. Hundreds? Maybe thousands? As they walked (or ran) to make their next fight, I envisioned that they would look up at Honest Abe, nod their heads, and agree with the message that he preached. *Absolutely*, they would think to themselves. *Our nation is a nation divided!*

And yet I—knowing that this quote was not actually Lincoln's—wondered what would happen if it was properly cited. What would happen if the poster showed a picture not of Lincoln, but of Jesus? Do we honestly think the response would be positive? Of course, it wouldn't. The same exact message—from the mouth of Jesus—would have created a public relations scandal.

The truth is, most people are on board with the ways of God—until they realize it is coming from God. They like the teachings but despise the Teacher. I have noticed a growing movement among the "self-development" crowd to worship something that they refer to as "source." Of course, these self-development types would never use the word *worship*, but they do make a point to use a capital *S*, thus betraying the reverence they pay to it.

When speaking about sources, energies, or even Mother Nature, the unbeliever is bowing to a "god" he created. He cherry-picks the things that he likes about God, and simply throws out the things that he does not. After running through his spiritual grocery list, the unbeliever decides to keep love, joy, forgiveness, and tolerance—and a universe that prioritizes him. At no point does this god make any commands of him, nor would it dare to deny him his wishes. That is why a "godless god" is so easy to worship. It requires nothing in return. It requires no change in lifestyle, tastes, schedules, or habits. It allows the unbeliever to check a box, call himself spiritual, and basically just do what he planned to do anyway. In this scenario, it is actually he—his

The truth is, most people are on board with the ways of God—until they realize it is coming from God. They like the teachings but despise the Teacher.

feelings, his emotions, his comforts, his desires—who has become the god of his life. As C. S. Lewis writes in *Mere Christianity*, "That is just why a vague religion—all about feeling God in nature, and so on—is so attractive. It is all thrills and no work."[10]

BE SEPARATE FROM THEM

While many Christians today try to be friends with the world, they must disobey the Bible to do so. From beginning to end, from Old Testament to New Testament, the Scriptures make it clear that God wants us to be separate. In the days before Jesus' birth, this separation was literal, physical, and relational in nature, with God forbidding the Israelites from marrying outside their nation. Today's separation, however, is an internal one, with God revealing His children by their obedient hearts. The apostle Paul said this to the Christians at Corinth:

> Do not be unequally yoked with unbelievers. For partnership has righteousness with lawlessness? Or what fellowship has light with darkness? What accord has Christ with Belial? Or what portion does a believer share with an unbeliever? What agreement has the temple of God with idols? For we are the temple of the living God. (2 Corinthians 6:14–16)

According to Paul, the God-fearing Christian—the true believer—is supposed to have no "partnership" or "fellowship" with unbelievers. The two do not mix. They are like oil and water or fire and ice. They have nothing in common in a spiritual sense. And why does Paul call us to such a stark separation? First, because Paul knows that any deep partnership (e.g., marriage, business, or friendship) that is built on opposing beliefs is simply a recipe for failure. It is only a matter of time before something blows up or something gives way. Second, Paul calls us to be separate from unbelievers because the New Covenant Christian—like the Old Testament Jew—is supposed to reflect God's image to a world that hates Him. We must remember our God is on a rescue mission. He plans to save this world and restore it to paradise. The people of the world, however, rebel against God at every turn. Knowing this to be the case, God uses human agents—the Christians who repent and obey His commandments—to reveal His character to the world.

In the Old Testament, God blessed the nation of Israel by giving them land, peace, and riches. When other nations saw this, they were forced to ponder the God of Israel. He was clearly more powerful than their idols of gold! Likewise, the New Testament Christian also carries God's blessing, but instead of giving us land and riches, God gives us our unity and love for each other. It was Jesus who said, "Just as I have loved you, you also are to love one another. By this all people will know that you are my disciples, if you have love for one another" (John 13:34–35).

In order for the world to notice God's image, there must be something different or abnormal to see. If the church were to allow premarital sex, foul language, drunkenness, selfish ambition, self-promotion, or any other lust that the world adores, then the world would start loving the church! The pews would be filled on a Sunday morning! However, they would get an image of God that is nowhere near real, which would lead them down a path to destruction.

God commands that Christians be separate. That is His plan, and that is His preference. You might be surprised that God would do such a thing. Is He not ignoring billions of people who do not call themselves "Christians"? Shouldn't everyone get a chance to receive God's blessings? In reality, the church's separation is not some evil scheme concocted by God to condemn the world. It is actually God's attempt to save it.

OTHERNESS

On the night Jesus was betrayed, He enjoyed one final meal with His closest friends. Jesus knew He would die the next morning, so He had some additional lessons to teach His disciples. But among the things that Jesus shared, there is one that was fairly unique—a prayer. It comes to us in John 17.

For over a dozen verses, Jesus prays to the Father to protect His disciples. This was not just a physical covering. It was much more a spiritual one. Jesus was more concerned with their minds and souls than He was with their physical bodies. But, as we study Jesus' prayer in John 17, you will notice that He makes a clear distinction—on numerous occasions—between His disciples and the people of the world. There was a dividing line between the two camps, and it was Jesus Himself who established it. Praying to God the Father, Jesus said:

> I have revealed Your name to the men whom You gave Me out of the world; they were Yours and You gave them to Me, and they have followed Your word . . . I ask on their behalf; I do not ask on behalf of the world, but on the behalf of those whom You have given Me, because they are Yours . . . I am not asking You to take them out of the world, but to keep them away from the evil one. They are not of the world, just as I am not of the world . . . I am not asking on behalf of these alone, but also for those who believe in Me through their word, that they may all be one; just as You, Father, are in Me and I in You, that they also may be in Us, so that the world may believe that You sent Me. (John 17:6, 9, 15–16, 20–21)

In this one prayer alone, we see Jesus refer to believers as "different" or "other" on multiple occasions. He says that His followers are those who are "given" to Him (v. 9), which implies that some men are *not* given to Him. We see Jesus proclaim that He is *not* praying for the unbelieving world (v. 9). We see Jesus say that His believers are "not of this world" (v. 16), again suggesting that other people *are* of this world. And then, to wrap it all up, Jesus tells us exactly why He is only praying for Christians. His reason? "So that the world may believe that You sent Me," He says (John 17:21).

The sanctification of the church is not some sort of human-focused, behind-closed-doors, "holier than thou" type of mission. It is the exact opposite. God has separated His church—and made her special—to make the world pay attention. Because of our otherness, our weirdness, our oddities as Christians, God is forcing the world to decide. *What do you actually believe about Jesus?* Our sanctification, therefore, is not just for us. It is also for the world around us.

> *The sanctification of the church is not some sort of human-focused, behind-closed-doors, "holier than thou" type of mission. God separated His church to make the world pay attention.*

THE WORLD OF TOMORROW

The United States of America was founded on a Judeo-Christian ethic. For nearly two hundred years, this biblical ethic was what Americans subscribed to. Almost everyone agreed on the importance of morality, chastity, worship, and prayer. It was easy to be a Christian in that version of America, but that is not the case today.

As our culture drifts away from that biblical ethic, the single-minded Christian will look increasingly different. We will look odd, strange, or unfit for society. We will be vilified and hated just for preaching the Bible. Our persecution will only accelerate as time goes by, and it is already occurring today. For example, when the coronavirus pandemic took America by storm, the marijuana dispensaries and liquor stores were deemed as "essential," but our churches were forced to lock their doors.[11] Likewise, under the Joe Biden administration, government prosecutors used the Freedom of Access to Clinic Entrances (FACE) Act to imprison pro-life activists who protested at abortion clinics. One such activist—a WWII concentration camp survivor—was nearly ninety years old at the time of her conviction.[12]

By sharing the black-and-white teachings of Scripture—like teachings on homosexuality, the creation of male and female, or anything else that the world finds offensive—we Christians will be subjects of government criticism. The question is, will we follow our God and obey His commandments, or will we play it safe, fall in line, and bow down to the world? As Jesus says in the gospel of John:

> If the world hates you, you know that it has hated Me before it hated you. If you were of the world, the world would love you as its own; but because you are not of the world, but I chose you out of the world, because of this the world hates you. (John 15:18–19 NASB)

So, if you ever feel weird, odd, or hated, if you ever feel like an outcast, if you ever feel misunderstood or disliked by the world, just know that means that you're probably doing this right. Truth be told, you *follow* an Outcast. You *worship* an Outcast.

You are made for a different world.

TODAY'S CHALLENGE

Answer the following questions:

In what way(s) are you choosing to be different from the world?

_____

_____

_____

_____

In what way(s) are you choosing to be the same as the world?

_____

_____

_____

_____

SOUL

YOUR SIN

If we say we have no sin, we deceive ourselves,
and the truth is not in us.
—1 JOHN 1:8

I was mortified. I thought I had kept it hidden. I had buried this artifact so deep, so far in the back of our garage, that I assumed that no one could find it. But sure enough, there it was, right in my buddy's hand. I was now in a world of trouble.

"What is this?" he asked.

"What is what?" I replied.

"This," he said, lifting his hand to eye height.

"Oh, that thing?" I answered. "Oh, well, I bought that in case I needed to, umm, grab something off the top shelf, or something."

He wasn't buying it. Frankly, I couldn't blame him. It made no sense for that thing to be in our garage. Nevertheless, he decided to drop the subject and just live with my lie. What was this thing I had hidden, you ask? Well, you are probably going to laugh at me when I say this, but it was a trash picker-upper. That's right, a trash picker-upper. You know, one of those plastic sticks with the claws on the end? Yeah, those things. Far from scandalous and far from exciting, but still a little embarrassing for a twenty-something-year-old man.

At that point in time, this friend and I were living in downtown Nashville. The house we were renting was beautiful, but it was located in a gentrifying area. The neighborhood was changing quickly. But even as I saw old houses being demolished and new houses being built, there was one problem about the neighborhood that never seemed to change: It was filthy. There was trash in the streets, trash on the sidewalks, and trash on the grass of the city parks. It was an endless sea of broken glass, fast-food wrappers, and cigarette butts. Admittedly, I was shocked that anyone could allow such conditions. Eventually, my unrest was so bad that I purchased the trash picker-upper, and then, my crusade began.

In the weeks that followed, I set out to *literally* clean up the streets. I awakened early in the morning, well before dawn, to seek and destroy the monster. Under the cover of darkness, I would walk through our neighborhood and pick up the garbage. In no time at all—maybe just thirty minutes—I could literally fill seven or eight bags worth of trash. Even though I dreaded being seen, I enjoyed the results. Little by little, street by street, the trash in the neighborhood vanished. The neighborhood was finally spick and span. But then, after a few weeks of work, I retired from duty and hung up the claw. I officially ended my trash picker-upping. Why? On that fateful morning—the morning of my retirement—I witnessed a scene that changed my thinking entirely.

It was trash day. As I heard the roar of the garbage truck off in the distance, I could not help but smile. *If these guys only knew*, I said to myself. Once the truck pulled up in front of our house, I watched the men jump out and start loading our cans. They threw load after load in their musty, steel cavern. But then, I noticed a detail that I had not before: they were actually spilling some trash. In fact, they were spilling a lot of trash. If a wrapper fell out, these guys would just leave it; if a bottle went flying, they would not chase it down. Even the machinery they used—the garbage truck itself—was perfectly constructed for measly results. On the bottom of their garbage truck was a hole, perhaps the size of a golf ball, that I imagine was there to let out the rainwater. The problem is, some pieces of trash are smaller than golf balls, which meant that trash also leaked from the hole.

—

Unless you address

the root of a problem,

that problem will

always persist.

—

As the truck pulled away, I watched a brown, putrid stream of sludge follow it into the distance. As I thought more about the scene I had just witnessed, I realized that all my early mornings, all those hours of work, had been acts of futility. My neighborhood would never be clean until the garbage men changed. Sure, the streets had seen a momentary improvement because of my work, but the problem remained unchanged. Unless you address the root of a problem, that problem will always persist. The lesson this taught me runs deeper than garbage. It also taught me about the nature of sin.

SETTING THE STANDARD

Most people will contend that human beings are born "good." When we say this, we often think of saints and citizens from our past—people like Mother Teresa, Abraham Lincoln, and Grandma. Our society stands in agreement—these folks are good people. But any measure of "goodness" is a measure of comparison. If we think ourselves to be good, then there must be someone or something that is decisively less good. How else could we know how we measure up?

If, for example, a man is over seven feet tall, then most people would say that man is tall. But when a person says something like, "Greg is tall," what they are really saying is, "Greg is tall compared to most humans." In that sense, they are absolutely right. Greg is certainly tall compared to most humans. If, however, we were to put Greg under the Empire State Building, then he would immediately become very small. Truthfully, objectively, small. Tallness and smallness, therefore—just like goodness and badness—are dependent on a standard of comparison. Greg is neither tall nor small until we compare him to something. It is the standard that determines his verdict.

And the same thing happens when we stand next to God.

Total Depravity

When we use God as our standard, our perspective on goodness will instantly change. God literally possesses an infinite goodness. His goodness, unlike the height of the Empire State Building, never comes to an end. It goes onward and upward to the corners of the space. Compared to God, the goodness of humans is quite unimpressive—yes, that even includes the goodness of Grandma. And yet, we humans have the gall to call ourselves good. When we call ourselves good, what we are really saying is, "I am good—*compared to most humans.*" But we are wretched compared to our God.

When it comes down to it, we humans are *not* born good. We are born as sinners and rebels and haters of God. It is only when we compare ourselves to God—not other human beings—that our corruption can make itself plain. Speaking of the nature of the fallen soul, the prophet Jeremiah once wrote, "The heart is deceitful above all things, and desperately sick; who can understand it?" (Jeremiah 17:9). Even the prophet Isaiah weighed in on the subject, saying that our most righteous deeds are like "filthy rags" (Isaiah 64:6 NIV). And if you think that these men are just talking about criminals, then the apostle Paul has a message for you. Writing to the Christians in Rome, he said:

There is none righteous, no, not one;
There is none who understands;
There is none who seeks after God.
They have all turned aside;
They have together become unprofitable;
There is none who does good, no, not one.
(Romans 3:10–12 NKJV)

Could Paul's words be any more inclusive? "There is none who does good," he says. To call ourselves good, therefore, we must ignore what the Bible says about us. The only way to get there is by ignoring God's standard. When a human being brags about his measure of goodness, he is conveniently forgetting the commands of the Bible. He is, in effect, standing under the Empire State Building, claiming to be tall, yet refusing to look up and face his reality. He does not look up, and consciously so, because he knows that he won't like the truth. It is safer for him to live with the lie. But it is exactly that—a lie. No human being is inherently good. It is actually quite the opposite. Here is what Jesus had to say about the human condition:

> *There is none who does good, no, not one.*
>
> —ROMANS 3:12 NKJV

> For from within, out of the hearts of people, come the evil thoughts, acts of sexual immorality, thefts, murders, acts of adultery, deeds of greed, wickedness, deceit, indecent behavior, envy, slander, pride, and foolishness. All these evil things come from within and defile the person. (Mark 7:21–23 NASB)

The apostle Paul added his take as well, sparing no words when addressing our sin:

> Now the works of the flesh are evident: sexual immorality, impurity, sensuality, idolatry, sorcery, enmity, strife, jealousy, fits of anger, rivalries, dissensions, divisions, envy, drunkenness, orgies, and things like these. (Galatians 5:19–21)

Only the humble of heart will face this reality. The single-minded Christian knows that his flesh is evil, wretched, and in need of cleansing (Romans 7:24). We are bad, not good, in our natural state. Therefore, it is not the vileness of the sinner that makes him different from the Christian; it is, in a word, his pride. He refuses to admit he is sinful and bad. This is why he chooses to live separated from God—he simply does not think that he needs Him. As C. S. Lewis reminds us:

> Christianity tells people to repent and promises them forgiveness. It therefore has nothing (as far as I know) to say to people who do not know they have done anything to repent of and who do not feel that they need any forgiveness.[13]

The Bible says that God is our standard of measure. Jesus said to His followers, "Be perfect, therefore, as your heavenly Father is perfect" (Matthew 5:48 NIV). But how can anyone reach such a height? How can anyone live a life of perfection? If God knows that we humans are incapable of perfection, why, you may ask, would God allow us to sin in the first place?

GOD'S PLAN FOR SIN

God hates sin. The Bible is clear about this. Because God is perfectly righteous and perfectly just, He hates rebellion and will punish all wrongs. There is one aspect of sin, however, that actually allows God to reveal more of His character. For example, when God forgives a sinner who is pleading for mercy, we are able to witness His capacity for mercy. This tells us something about God's nature. While He does seek justice, He is also able to delay His judgments and pardon the sinner. We could not witness this happening without the man's sin. So, while God does hate all sin, that sin still allows us to witness His mercies (Psalm 51:1; 1 Chronicles 21:13).

When Jesus died on the cross, He willingly accepted God's wrath in our place. Remember: God is still a righteous judge, which means every single sin will be punished eventually. In a good justice system, this must be the case. Each of those debts—or sins, as we call them—will be paid by one debtor of record. Either we can pay the debt that we rightfully owe, or Jesus can pay it instead. He offers us that choice. Because Jesus was despised, we can be welcomed. Because Jesus became dirty, we can be clean.

It is through this simple act of accepting God's offer that our hearts can be made good. Once we allow Jesus to cover our debt, there is no more broken glass, cigarette butts, or filthy sludge on our ledger. But in order to experience the joy of this cleansing, we must first face the truth of our sinfulness. We have to admit that we are dirty, rotten, and wretched. We have to admit that we're truly *not* good—not on our own, that is. The first step in that process is repentance from sin. We must see it, admit it, and turn away from it—all of which is made possible by the help of the Holy Spirit. It is only then that we can live a life of obedience, joy, and service to others.

—

Because Jesus was despised, we can be welcomed. Because Jesus became dirty, we can be clean.

—

Until we address the root of a problem, that problem will always persist.

Our problem is sin, and Christ is the answer.

TODAY'S CHALLENGE

Step 1:
Read the following verses about God's forgiveness:

> Whoever conceals his transgressions will not prosper,
> but he who confesses and forsakes them will obtain
> mercy. (Proverbs 28:13)

> If we confess our sins, he is faithful and just to forgive
> us our sins and to cleanse us from all unrighteous-
> ness. (1 John 1:9)

Step 2:
Spend some time in private reflection. How might you be
living in sin these days? (Do you use foul language? Do you
drink yourself drunk once the workweek is over? Do you
dress in sensual clothing to draw attention to yourself? Are
you consistently jealous of the lives of others?) Write them
down here:

_____

_____

_____

Step 3:
Confess those sins to God. See the wrong in them, commit to
stopping them, and ask God to remove your debt for them.
And then, after you have repented, delight in God's mercy
and goodness, because you know that you are forgiven!

DAY ELEVEN

YOUR PRIDE

Pride goes before destruction, and a haughty spirit before a fall.
—PROVERBS 16:18

I n the first few months of my professional life, there were two papers that graced my desk. Prominently displayed, there was no way I could miss them as I sat down to work. (Nor could anyone else as they passed by my cubicle.) These papers served as reminders. They were my fuel, my motivation, for success. I both loved them and hated them at the same time. The first paper said this:

Dear Bob,

Enclosed, please find the MLB — Notice of Disposition stating that you have been unconditionally released from the Toronto Blue Jays Baseball Club. Please sign & date the field marked with a red "x" and return in the self-addressed envelope.

Best wishes in your future pursuits.

With its iconic Blue Jays logo in the top left corner, this letter served as a reminder of two difficult years. I had scratched and clawed to get to the Big Leagues, but I had failed. I didn't make it. And so, I resolved to never forget the words of that letter. I wanted to show everyone with the Toronto Blue Jays—and probably myself—that I was not a failure.

The second letter on my desk was nearly identical. It said:

Dear Mr. Wheatley,

In accordance with the provisions of Article XIX, sections B and C of the Minor League Uniform Player Contract (hereinafter "UPC"), the St. Louis Cardinals, LLC hereby notifies you its decision to terminate on this date the UPC signed by the parties.

Sincerely, Minor League Operations, St. Louis Cardinals

To some people in my office, these papers might have seemed impressive. If they walked by my desk and saw those letterheads, I hoped that they would think, *Oh, this desk belongs to a professional athlete! I wonder who it might be.* These papers, therefore, were not just used for personal motivation. They were also used as a fuel for my pride. Plain and simple, I wanted people to think I was awesome. I hoped that their praise would erase my insecurities. But if the seasoned Christian had walked by my desk, they would have known the truth of the matter. That desk did not belong to a professional athlete, a financial advisor, or a first-year associate who was trying to hustle. Oh no.

That desk belonged to a prideful man.

THE TRUTH ABOUT PRIDE

Pride is the deepest form of insecurity. It is a mirage. Though the prideful man expresses confidence, strength, and competence outwardly, he is deeply afraid of the thing he knows inwardly. A prideful man is not confident; he is searching. He is a magician, a con man, a professional distractor and concealer of truth. Because he does not know (or like) who he is, he uses others as a standard to measure his status. *Surely, I am smarter than Philip*, he thinks. *And I am clearly more handsome than Brandon*, he adds.

Pride is the deepest form of insecurity. A prideful man is not confident; he is searching.

What the prideful man refuses to see is that his thinking is flawed and short-sighted. By seeking to find value within himself, he enlists in an endless crusade. Because he has chosen to be a slave of comparison, he needs new and fresh versions of Philip and Brandon. He will always be searching to find lesser humans. C. S. Lewis put it this way:

> Pride gets no pleasure out of having something, only out of having more of it than the next man. We say that people are proud of being rich, or clever, or good-looking, but they are not. They are proud of being richer, or cleverer, or better-looking than others. If everyone else became equally rich, or clever, or good-looking there would be nothing to be proud about. It is the comparison that makes you proud: the pleasure of being above the rest.[14]

And this was exactly my sin with those letters on my desk. While I certainly used them for motivation, I also used them to peacock before others. I was, in my own, subtle way, trying to assert my dominance within the office. Because I had been a professional athlete, I thought that I had something to hang over my coworkers. *I am on a different level* was the message I was trying to send. Admittedly, my behavior in those days was more boyish than manly, and I had yet to grasp how much God hates our pride. The Bible repeatedly affirms that God opposes the proud. But how, exactly, does God oppose us?

GOD OPPOSES THE PROUD

As offensive as this may sound, the Bible actually teaches that we are born as the children of Satan. That's right. We are born as children of the prince of darkness. It is only through an adoption process that we can become the children of God. Just like our birth father, the devil, it is in our nature to fluff up our feathers. We love to be seen as wise, attractive, successful, and important. Even more so, we want to believe that we've earned those gifts. It is because of *our* work and *our* good decisions that success has rained from the heavens. If we are rich, famous, intelligent, or successful, it is because *we* have done the right things. *Our* name is stamped on the trophies of life.

This is a common theme in the heart of a sinner, and it has been since the fall of man. Even in Old Testament times, as the Israelites were entering the Promised Land, God issued them a warning against harboring pride. He said:

> Beware that you do not forget the Lord your God by not keeping His commandments, His judgments, and His statutes which I command you today, lest—when you have eaten and are full, and have built beautiful houses and dwell in them; and when your herds and your flocks multiply, and your silver and your gold are multiplied, and all that you have is multiplied . . . then you say in your heart, "My power

and the might of my hand have gained me this wealth."
(Deuteronomy 8:11–13, 17 NKJV)

My power. My hand. My wealth. There are the words of a prideful heart. While God could never feel insecure or be robbed of glory, the Bible does portray Him as a jealous God. In Deuteronomy 4:24, God is described as "a consuming fire, a jealous God." In Exodus 34:14, the Bible even says that God's name is "Jealous." This theme of the Bible is clear and consistent: God does not share the spotlight with anyone. As God says Himself in the book of Isaiah, "I am the LORD, that is My name; I will not give My glory to another" (Isaiah 42:8 NASB).

Why, then, does God hate pride? Why does God oppose the proud? Put simply, God opposes the proud because He alone deserves glory. It is His power, His might, and His wealth that He gives us. Everything begins with the hand of God. This is why God is so militant when we step into pride. He wants us to see Him, know Him, and love Him, and He knows that our pride can prevent that from happening.

The less pride we have, the more God we get. This has been God's design from the very beginning.

GOD GIVES GRACE TO THE HUMBLE

In the early days of Solomon's reign, God visited the young king in a dream. In that dream, God said to Solomon, "Ask for whatever you want me to give you" (1 Kings 3:5 NIV). Solomon, knowing that he was young and not qualified to lead, asked God to grant him wisdom. This pleased God very much. As a result, God decided not only to give Solomon wisdom, but also to give him things that he did not request— things like riches, honor, and a blossoming empire. Solomon soon became the wisest man in the world

The less pride we have,

the more God we get.

(1 Kings 3:12). Even still, the life of Solomon saw a tragic ending, proving that all the world's wisdom cannot prevent sin.

In Deuteronomy 17:16–17, God commanded that any king of Israel should not multiply horses, wives, gold, or silver. God wanted Israel's kings to trust in Him, not in military prowess (horses), strategic political marriages (wives), or accumulating wealth (through gold and silver). Solomon went on to commit all three of these sins. The Bible records that Solomon had forty thousand stalls of horses (1 Kings 4:26), seven hundred wives (1 Kings 11:3), and riches like we could not imagine. In fact, the book of 2 Chronicles even says that Solomon was so rich that "Nothing was made of silver, because silver was considered of little value in Solomon's day" (2 Chronicles 9:20 NIV).

Why do I share all this with you? Why tell this story of riches to rags? Well, by the end of Solomon's life, he was no longer walking with God. By doing what was evil in the eyes of the Lord, his heart turned away from serving the Lord (1 Kings 11:6, 9). The wisest man who had ever lived forgot to remember his God. And what caused Solomon to go astray? You guessed it. *Pride.* Solomon fell in love with his gifts—his power, his wives, the advice that they gave him (1 Kings 11:4)—and he ignored the commands of the Giver. Instead of listening to God and following His lead, Solomon decided to live for himself.

I have often wondered: How would I respond if God gave me that wish? If God visited me in a dream, giving me the same deal that He offered to Solomon, what gift would I ask for? What would you choose if you were given the chance? In my estimation, I think that the wisest choice (no pun intended) would be if we asked for humility. Yes, as boring and anticlimactic as that may sound, humility would be the thing that I'd ask God to grant me. Even though God praised Solomon when he asked for wisdom, the fruit of his life became terribly sour. This tells me that there might have been a better choice. While it might appear that asking for humility means asking for less,

I would actually argue the opposite. It is only once we can say, "Lord, You are my everything," that God can bless us without reservation. It is then, and not before, that His secondary blessings are no longer a threat. In the words of F. B. Meyer:

> I used to think that God's gifts were on shelves—one above another—and the taller we grow, the easier we can reach them. Now I find that God's gifts are on shelves—and the lower we stoop, the more we get.[15]

The humble Christian receives love, joy, and peace in his life. Why? Because the humble Christian has God in his life. Oddly enough, if we chose the seemingly boring, anticlimactic gift of humility, we receive the greatest gift of all: Jesus Christ, Himself. Therefore, living a life of humility not only honors God but also accomplishes the best end for us. This is why the Bible so strongly encourages a heart of humility, often saying things like:

> *It is only once we can say, "Lord, You are my everything," that God can bless us without reservation.*

> Whoever exalts himself will be humbled, and whoever humbles himself will be exalted. (Matthew 23:12)

> Humble yourselves, therefore, under the mighty hand of God so that at the proper time he may exalt you. (1 Peter 5:6)

> Though the LORD is on high, yet He regards the lowly; but the proud He knows from afar. (Psalm 138:6 NKJV)

What a horrible thing to be known from afar! The single-minded Christian should fear such a distance. But therein lies our true motivation: We foster humility to be closer to God. By falling at His feet, He lifts us to ours. We are seen; we are validated; we are loved. This is the very place that our hearts are searching for. Our hearts long to be exalted and seen.

The prideful heart wants to be seen by men.

The humble heart is seen by God.

TODAY'S CHALLENGE

The prideful heart says, "I deserve _____ (e.g., justice, revenge, a raise, a spouse)." How might you be answering that question today?

Step 1: Fill in the blank.

I deserve _____.

_____.

_____.

_____.

Step 2:

Spend some time in reflection and prayer. Ask God to forgive you for your moments of pride, and ask Him to help you draw closer to Him.

DAY TWELVE

YOUR PAIN

In this world you will have trouble
—JOHN 16:33 NIV

During my professional baseball career, I would spend every offseason in Covington, Louisiana. Just thirty minutes north of New Orleans, Covington is a quaint little city filled with kind, southern families. But as much as I enjoyed my time in the bayou, I would always remember my reason for being there. I did not go for the jazz music, oysters, or Café du Monde. I went to get better at baseball. When you are a minor league player without a Major League contract, the next spring training could always be your last.

Why Louisiana, you ask? Well, Covington played host to a world-class pitching coach, and this man had proven results. I was surrounded by Big Leaguers constantly. We were in the gym for eight hours a day, Monday through Friday, like clockwork. I knew that if I could train with some of the best athletes in the world, then my abilities would be pushed to their limit.

I usually spent four months with this coach, stepping under his guidance from November to February. His program was second to none, but it was not cheap. I paid this coach thousands of dollars a

—

All pain is painful, but

not all pain is harmful.

—

year for his tutelage (which, for a minor league player making $1,100 per month, was about all I had at the time.) Nevertheless, I believed in this coach and his methods, and I steadily improved each year. But my fastball is not the point of this story. The point of this story is pain.

The truth of the matter is, I paid this coach thousands of dollars a year to hurt me. I specifically hired him to hurt me with purpose. Through his workouts and challenges (and insane dinner menus), he was helping me achieve a result. What I learned in Louisiana was this simple lesson:

All pain is painful, but not all pain is harmful.

THE PRESENCE OF PAIN

When addressing the topic of pain, the first thing we must do is recognize its reality. Pain exists. While some of our days might be better than others, no one goes through life without experiencing pain. The pain we suffer might be due to a death in the family, an illness, a natural disaster, or even our own decisions, but the reality of pain cannot be ignored. But because pain is uncomfortable, many people do their best to avoid it completely.

This "pain avoidance" is not entirely wrong, per se, because some pain is there to alert us to danger. For example, if your hand starts to hurt when it rests on the stove, then that pain is valuable feedback. Your hand is burning, and it must be removed! You are better and safer on account of that pain. However, the kind of pain that can pull us from God has little to do with our bodies. This pain is a pain of the mind and soul, and it is more properly defined as *suffering*. Suffering is simply pain, continued. It is pain, prolonged. The sinful heart is most angry at God when it is forced to walk through suffering. When we are suffering, we begin to question our loyalty to Him, and His to us. *How could God let this happen?* we think. *Couldn't God have prevented this hardship?*

This is a very human response, of course, but it is forgetting God's hand in our suffering. The Bible makes this clear: It is not that God ignores our suffering—it is He, in fact, who allows it. God is the Author of our story. There is nothing that resides outside His control, even the things that appear "bad" on the surface.

Though this fact might seem crass, it is a theme that is often repeated in Scripture. For example, God rhetorically asked through the mouth of Amos, "When disaster comes to a city, has not the LORD caused it?" (Amos 3:6 NIV). And through the prophet Jeremiah, God said, "Is it not from the mouth of the Most High that good and bad come?" (Lamentations 3:38). And finally, God brought His point home through the hand of Isaiah, saying, "I am the LORD, and there is no other. I form the light and create darkness, I bring prosperity and create disaster; I, the LORD, do all these things" (Isaiah 45:6–7 NIV).

What an incredibly humbling statement that is. Here is our all-loving Father, openly admitting that He does "all these things." He brings both prosperity and disaster, both good times and bad. This image of God disrupts our assumptions. Because we are told that "God is good all the time," we assume that His work will always be pleasurable. According to C. S. Lewis, "We want, in fact, not so much a Father in heaven as a grandfather in heaven—a senile benevolence who, as they say, 'liked to see young people enjoying themselves.'"[16]

Let me ask you this: Do you think there were tornadoes in the Garden of Eden? How about famines? Murders? Shoplifting or shark attacks? You, of course, know the answer is no. If Adam and Eve had never sinned—which you and I are guilty of every day—then there would be no pain and suffering on this planet. While God does ordain that bad things will happen, we must remember what causes these things. Mankind is the one that spoiled this world, and that spoiling has brought us much pain. Therefore, the pains that we suffer are the result of *our* actions, nothing more.

The good news is, our Master knows the purpose of pain.

THE PURPOSE OF PAIN

God does not create sin, but He does allow suffering. The Bible makes this clear: God, not Satan, is the bringer of calamity. If Satan is the hammer, then God is the hand. Because God is the ultimate bringer of pain, that means that He always does so with a purpose. God wills our chastening, our strengthening, and our advancement toward holiness, and pain is one instrument for doing it. This theme consistently appears throughout the pages of Scripture, appearing in both the Old and New Testaments alike. In the Old Testament, for example, God said this to the Jews in the wilderness:

> And you shall remember that the Lord your God led you all the way these forty years in the wilderness, to humble you and test you, to know what was in your heart, whether you would keep His commandments or not. So He humbled you, allowed you to hunger, and fed you with manna which you did not know nor did your fathers know, that He might make you know that man shall not live by bread alone; but man lives by every word that proceeds from the mouth of the Lord. (Deuteronomy 8:2–3 NKJV)

If Satan is the hammer, then God is the hand.

God did not take the Israelites through the wilderness because it was pleasurable. He took them to the wilderness because it was hard. (You will notice that He took them to the desert, not to some beach on the Mediterranean.) He shaped their character by making them suffer. He was changing His people through intentional pain, and God does the same with you and me. Perhaps our pain is induced through an illness, an irreplaceable loss, or a season of unchanging circumstances. In seasons such as these, we may feel like God is distant or, even worse, evil. We feel stuck. We feel desperate. This is where true suffering begins because we realize our lack of control. But the writer of Hebrews takes the opposite stance, actually praising God and His purpose for suffering. He encouraged the Hebrews with these words:

> It is for discipline that you have to endure. God is treating you as sons. For what son is there whom his father does not discipline? . . . Besides this, we have had earthly fathers who disciplined us and we respected them. Shall we not much more be subject to the Father of spirits and live? For they disciplined us for a short time as it seemed best to them, but he disciplines us for our good, that we may share his holiness. For the moment all discipline seems painful rather than pleasant, but later it yields the peaceful fruit of righteousness to those who have been trained by it. (Hebrews 12:7, 9–11)

Like an earthly father would discipline his children, God uses our pain to improve our character. No child is born with maturity or holiness, which means that we have to be taught such things. For the single-minded Christian, God's discipline is still painful, but it is far from harmful. We are being shaped into the image of Jesus each day. As the apostle Paul so famously wrote:

> And we know that all things work together for good to those who love God, to those who are called according to His purpose. For whom He foreknew, He also predestined to be

conformed to the image of His Son, that He might be the firstborn among many brethren. (Romans 8:28–29 NKJV)

THE PLEASURE OF PAIN

All pain is painful, but not all pain is harmful. It is the end result of our pain—or the character of He who inflicts it—that should dictate our response to that pain. Our willingness to endure our pain and suffering, therefore, is always in proportion to our expected gain. This is why Peter could say:

> Beloved, do not be surprised at the fiery trial when it comes upon you to test you, as though something strange were happening to you. But rejoice insofar as you share Christ's sufferings, that you may also rejoice and be glad when his glory is revealed. (1 Peter 4:12–13)

Likewise, the apostle James added:

> Consider it pure joy, my brothers and sisters, whenever you face trials of many kinds, because you know that the testing of your faith produces perseverance. Let perseverance finish its work so that you may be mature and complete, not lacking anything. (James 1:2–4 NIV)

And finally, the apostle Paul concluded:

> Not only that, but we rejoice in our sufferings, knowing that suffering produces endurance, and endurance produces character, and character produces hope. (Romans 5:3–4)

To Peter, James, and Paul, a season of pain was actually a blessing. They had a godly perspective on how to treat suffering. Just look at the fruits they said suffering could offer: rejoicing, gladness, perseverance, maturity, completeness, endurance, character, hope. If those are the things that suffering produces, then one might be tempted to be grateful for suffering!

Our pain makes us like Christ, and our pain puts us near Christ. It is this union, perhaps, that is the greatest reward of our suffering. The writer of Hebrews says that even Jesus was forced to suffer on earth, both to strengthen His character and to connect with us sinners. He writes:

> For it was fitting for Him, for whom are all things and by whom are all things, in bringing many sons to glory, to make the captain of their salvation perfect through sufferings . . . Therefore, in all things He had to be made like His brethren, that He might be a merciful and faithful High Priest in things pertaining to God, to make propitiation for the sins of the people. For in that He Himself has suffered, being tempted, He is able to aid those who are tempted. (Hebrews 2:10, 17–18 NKJV)

While suffering is guaranteed in the life of a sinner, Jesus Himself was not a sinner. This means that Jesus suffered, willingly, so He could meet us in our seasons of pain. This means that our pain, in a sense, gives us yet another avenue to have friendship with Christ. If we ever feel lonely or abandoned, we can cry out to the One who was left by His friends. If we ever feel falsely accused, mistreated, or misunderstood, we can pray to the One who was killed for no crime.

We often commit sin when we try to avoid suffering. Have you noticed? When the truth is

Our pain makes us like Christ, and our pain puts us near Christ.

painful, we lie. When forgiveness is difficult, we maintain a grudge. Because pain is painful, we do everything we can to avoid it. The single-minded Christian, however, understands that God uses suffering to expel our impurities. On the day when we finally see our Lord, we will thank Him for our moments of suffering. We will be conformed to the character of Christ, and we will know that our pain has been worth it.

All pain is painful.

But not all pain is harmful.

TODAY'S CHALLENGE

Fill in the blanks.

I am feeling pain in these areas:

Which means God could be accomplishing:

_____ _____

_____ _____

_____ _____

_____ _____

_____

YOUR EMOTIONS

A time to weep, and a time to laugh; a time to mourn, and a time to dance.
—ECCLESIASTES 3:4

I t was time to put my money where my mouth was. After several weeks of vetting, I finally, officially said yes to this vendor. We had some pretty audacious goals to conquer, and both sides were excited to begin our partnership.

During my onboarding process with this new vendor, I noticed the slightest of clerical errors. (They were using the wrong email address for me, so I was not getting the necessary materials.) While the issue was not life-altering, it still needed to be remedied in a timely manner. Naturally, I reached out to the person who handled such things, and I asked them to make the adjustment.

And I got no response.

Waiting about a week or so, I tried to connect with this person again. Still, no response. Then, I tried it a third time—this time through a different medium—and still, I received no reply. At this point, several weeks had gone by with the unaddressed problem. Not only that, but even my attempts to fix it had gone unacknowledged. I was angry.

Long story short, the error was eventually addressed. There were many strongly worded emails that had died in my drafts folder. Just a few weeks later, I met this person face-to-face, and she was both apologetic and kind. My whining and wailing made me feel very small. I was humbled. Later that night, I wrote this in my journal:

> *I continue to be amazed at how wretched I am. Over the past few weeks, I've been increasingly frustrated with (name) from (company). I became so angry that I nearly sent her a scathing email, telling her that "I deserved better" and how disappointed I was. Luckily, I decided otherwise, because then came today—my first official meeting with (company). When I saw (name), she immediately apologized to me. The day went incredibly well, and that never would have happened if I had been a jerk over email. I thought like a jerk, I punched out those emails like one, but I did not act upon it. Quick to listen; slow to speak; slow . . . to . . . anger.*

In our selfish, fallen natures, our emotions are often not aligned with reality. We have a wonderful way of catastrophizing things. Our emotions can sometimes lie to us. While our emotions are gifts from God that can help us relate to Him, they, too, have been warped by the Fall. Therefore, because our emotions have been contaminated by sin, we must learn to root them in the truth. It was a valuable lesson that I had to learn.

THE ISOLATION OF EMOTION

In my first book, *Our Hearts' Desire*, I shared briefly about a personal season of disappointment. It was a difficult time in my life, and there were plenty of emotions that came with it. During this time, there was a mentor in my life who was especially comforting. In one respect, I was relieved to have someone to talk to, but in another, no amount of words ever seemed to fulfill me. The words just seemed to run on and on. The emotions just did not stop.

Our emotions are a vehicle to grow closer to Him.

When I asked her why I had so much to say, she just looked at me and smiled. She obviously had seen this occurrence before. "The heart knows its own bitterness," she said in reply, "and no stranger shares its joy" (quoting Proverbs 14:10). She went on to explain the message of this verse: The heart, in its deepest moments of joy and sadness, will often exist in isolation. Even though we might be surrounded by people, the cries of our hearts are uniquely our own. This is why we say things like, "I can't possibly express the joy that I feel!" or, "Words can't express our sadness for Tom." We say these things because they are true. Our words do, in fact, fall short. In the deepest recesses of our hearts, we are somewhat inaccessible to our fellow man. And yet, we want to be known and understood completely. So where, then, do our emotions lead us? How can this "isolation" actually serve us?

Like so many other things that God created, our emotions are a vehicle to grow closer to Him. You will notice that it is the "stranger" who does not share our joy, but God is far more than a stranger. In fact, the Bible makes it clear that God lives, quite literally, inside of our hearts. He says:

> I will give you a new heart and put a new spirit in you; I will remove from you your heart of stone and give you a heart of flesh. (Ezekiel 36:26 NIV)

> Or do you not know that your body is a temple of the Holy Spirit within you, whom you have from God? (1 Corinthians 6:19)

The Spirit of God lives inside us. There is no distance, no separation, no relating to strangers in our relationship with Him. Our relationship with God is not merely one of closeness or spiritual proximity—our relationship with God is defined by oneness. Our emotions are a way we can access that oneness.

Humans are relational and born for connection. We want to be seen, known, heard, and loved. We want to matter to someone who matters to us. In our moments of sadness, fatigue, and disappointment, the human experience has failed us. Life on this earth leaves us wanting for more. In those moments that we feel our deepest pain, our words are not vanities filling the air; they are simply our cries for help. They beckon for the thing we were always made for: a sinless oneness with God.

THE HEART OF WORSHIP

As previously stated, our emotions can help us draw closer to God. Thus, emotions have their place in worship. We should not try to stifle our emotions, but we also should not let them run wild. Our mind, not our heart, is the captain of this ship. Therefore, we must put our emotions in their rightful place, rooting them in the truths of the Bible.

The conservative church often appeals to our knowledge. This is a good thing. We need knowledge. While the first step is to read, learn, and take hold of God's truths, the second step is to feel a reaction. God's truths are meant to exact a response! First, we learn a truth and store it away, and then, we feel something wonderful. (We experience love, joy, gratitude, reverence, and so on.) By reading, learning, and internalizing God's Word, we give ourselves anchors to hold onto. It is these anchors of truth that produce real emotions. We must remember that even God Himself experiences emotions. This is the very same God who experienced love (John 3:16), hate (Psalm 5:5), joy (Isaiah 62:5), sadness (Genesis 6:6), jealousy (Exodus 34:14), and pity (Judges 2:18) in the Scriptures. As God's imagers on earth, reflecting His name, we too should experience these emotions.

God's strength makes us feel safe.

God's wrath makes us feel fear.

God's gifts make us feel joy.

God's plan makes us feel peace.

That is the point of reading Scripture. By understanding God's character on an intimate level, our emotions can respond accordingly. They are the payoff that we Christians receive. God does not want us to stop at simply reading, learning, and knowing about Him. He wants us to experience that reality! Our emotions are the payoff when God's truths take hold of us.

Our emotions are the fruit of understanding. They are meant to be the overflow of a relationship with God. It is for this reason that I created the concept below, which I call the "Tree of Worship."

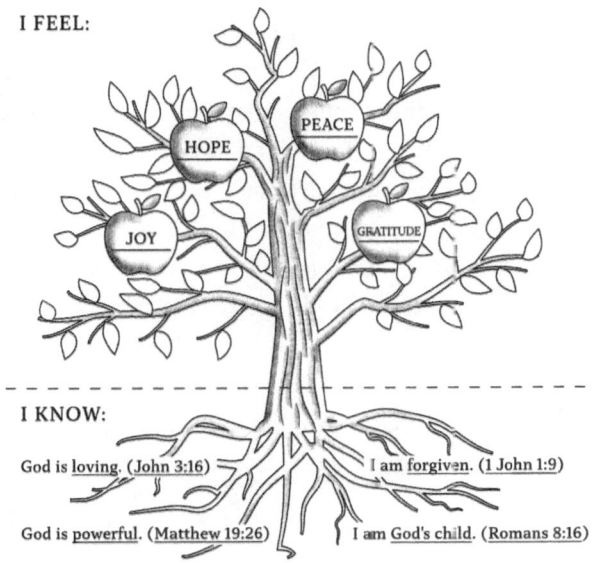

—

Our knowledge is the root of our worship, and our emotions are the fruit of our worship.

—

As you will notice, both knowledge and emotions are required for worship. It is because of what we know (e.g., God is loving, I am forgiven, and so on) that we can feel joy, hope, and peace with accuracy. In other words, our knowledge is the root of our worship, and our emotions are the fruit of our worship. If we lack either component, then true worship ceases. Knowledge without emotion will lead us to legalism, and emotion without knowledge will lead us to heresy. Both omissions can distort our thoughts about God, but true worship is restored with their balance.

The Gift of Emotions

Perhaps you've been blessed with abundant emotions. You are all emotions, all the time. You laugh, you cry, you sing, you dance. You emote. This, to be sure, is a good part of you (when wisdom is also engaged).

On the other side of the coin, perhaps you have taught yourself to hide your emotions. You feel safer and stronger by keeping them in. Let me say this: Your emotions are not a mistake, my friend. They are gifts from the God who also emotes. He created you to be like Him.

You might be the stoic who is learning to emote, or you might be the hysteric who is learning God's truths. Either way, your emotions are a way to connect you with God. As He works to perfect your emotions, He will use them to draw you to Him. The wise King Solomon was exactly right—the heart does, in fact, know its own bitterness, and no stranger can share in its joy.

But God can.

Today's Challenge

Fill out your own Tree of Worship.

First, find some truths in the Bible that are the <u>root</u> of your worship (include the Bible verses for future reference). Second, describe your corresponding emotions as the <u>fruit</u> of your worship.

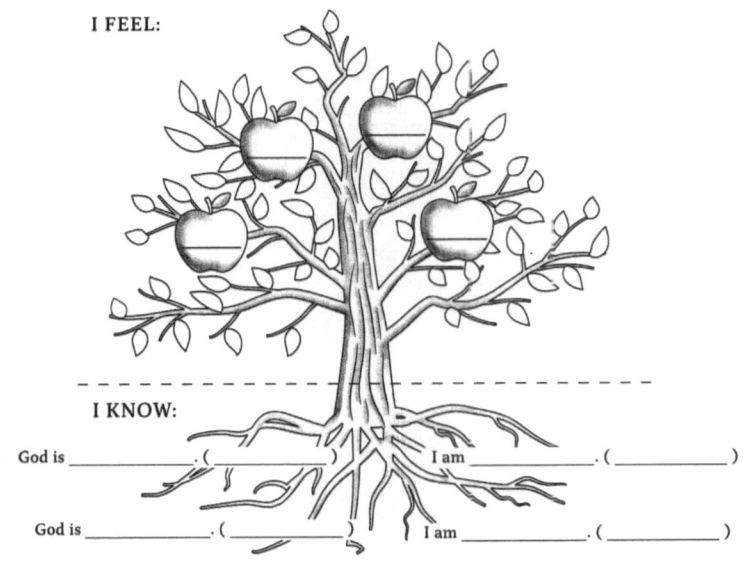

I FEEL:

I KNOW:

God is _____ . (_____)   I am _____ . (_____)

God is _____ . (_____)   I am _____ . (_____)

YOUR LONELINESS

Turn to me and be gracious to me, for I am lonely and afflicted.
—PSALM 25:16

I f you have been single for a significant period of time, then you are likely well acquainted with loneliness. As one who is wired to work and a natural introvert, I, too, have faced my fair share of loneliness.

While all humans can feel a sense of loneliness, most single people face a double dose. Some Christians are born with the gift of celibacy (as we discussed in detail on Day Five), but the majority of us desire to be married. It is this crowd that agrees with God's words in the Garden of Eden, where He said, "It is not good for the man to be alone" (Genesis 2:18 NIV). And yet, we are alone. We still remain single. Why, then, has God let us linger in our season of singleness? If it is not good for man to be alone, then why has God not brought us a spouse? We singles, like the psalmist before us, cry out:

> How long, Lord? Will You forget me forever?
> How long will You hide Your face from me?
> How long am I to feel anxious in my soul,
> With grief in my heart all the day? (Psalm 13:1–2 NASB)

As we covered just two days ago, all pain is painful, but not all pain is harmful. Our loneliness is an example of such pain.

LEARNING TO LOVE

Many Christians fail to realize this truth about love: It is in love's absence that we learn to appreciate it. It is only when our desires go unmet for extended periods of time that we can fully come to grips with these longings. We see this unfold in other facets of life, like when someone is fasting from food. It is in the absence of food that our cravings are piqued. When you go a day or two without food, your relationship with food immediately changes. It goes from a menial want to a literal need, and it quickly becomes your priority. And then, once you are given some food and break your fast, you are primed and ready to receive it. You appreciate that food more than ever before. You cherish it. You are grateful.

An absence of love has this very effect. In a similar way to fasting, an absence of love is a life-threatening event. I am not being facetious or hyperbolic; I am speaking in a literal sense. When you have less love, you have less life. A methodical death is a death nonetheless. As it says in Proverbs 17:22, "A joyful heart is good medicine, but a crushed spirit dries up the bones." With anxiety, depression, and suicide on the rise, the evidence reveals that we are in a crisis of loneliness. Our emotional state does affect our bodies. But then again, a fast will affect our bodies too. Perhaps when our stomach growls—or, in this case, when our heart is lonely—it is sounding the alarm to an absence of love. It is this alarm that awakens us to our needs.

HUMBLE, LOWLY, AND FULLY ALIVE

There is a sense in which Christians are the loneliest of all. Because the Christian's heart is fully awake, it is fully aware of its unmet needs. Our hearts need to be loved, wholly and consistently, and the lonely heart does not feel enough love. We also have an adverse relationship with fleshly vices, rendering sex or drugs as untenable options. For many singles, the feeling of loneliness seems like a terrible thing, but Jesus had a different take. He said this in His sermon on the mount:

> Blessed are the poor in spirit, for theirs is the kingdom of heaven. Blessed are those who mourn, for they shall be comforted. Blessed are the meek, for they shall inherit the earth. (Matthew 5:3–5)

On the surface, one might think these are all bad things. Who would ever want to be poor in spirit? Who would ever choose to be meek and mourning? Evidently, Jesus. Jesus would want to be meek and mourning. The everyday human does not think this way. In our flesh, we want to be lofty, strong, and happy. We want to experience comfort, and we want comfort now.

So why does Jesus say that the poor, meek, and mourning are blessed? Well, the only reason that Jesus could say such a thing was because of His eternal perspective. He was setting His mind on things above. When a person is poor in spirit and meek and mourning, he becomes fully aware of his need for God's love. With an extreme absence of earthly pleasures, the lonely heart will cry out to God. *Save me. Help me*, our souls seem to say. We then turn to the Lord and look forward to heaven.

It is in this sense that our loneliness serves us. When we are faced with an extended season of loneliness, we come face-to-face with our deepest need. The human heart was made to be loved, just as the stomach was made to hold food. In an absence of food, the stomach will growl; in an absence of love, the Christian seeks God.

THE HUMAN CONDITION

The human race was made in the image of God, meant to be fully connected and tethered to Him. We were never made to be alone. The problem is, ever since the fall in the Garden of Eden, we have been alone. In fact, one might even say that loneliness is now the human condition. As C. S. Lewis once wrote, "We are born helpless. As soon as we are fully conscious we discover loneliness."[17]

We were created to be loved all the time. There should never be a gap in our sense of belonging. This world, however, creates plenty of gaps. While plenty of marriages are rife with loneliness, it is the single person—with no plans or prospects on a Friday night—who comes face-to-face with this plight most often. It is perfectly clear to the single person that we do not have the love that we need, but unfortunately, this gap is less clear to those in relationships. They have just enough comfort (or plans, or distractions) that they can turn a blind eye to reality. As King Solomon once wrote, "A satisfied soul loathes the honeycomb, but to a hungry soul every bitter thing is sweet" (Proverbs 27:7 NKJV). What Solomon is saying is that the man with much grows bored of his luxuries, but the poor man rejoices over the tiniest pleasure. This is where our loneliness—our relational hunger—can actually help us find love. This is why Jesus could say that it is better to mourn on earth than it is to feel pleasure—it keeps our eyes on the prizes of heaven. There are plenty of people, however, who have very little desire for

—

In an absence of food,

the stomach will growl;

in an absence of love,

the Christian seeks God.

—

heaven or God. Why? Because they think that they have everything they need already. They have houses, spouses, children, and jobs. They take a trip to the lake every August. They experience sex and romance. For the most part, things are good for people like that. There is no major gap for them to ask God to meet, so He has few avenues through which He can enter.

But this is not true for the poor man.

When God is all you have, you will learn He is all you need. I do not mean that God can fulfill every longing on earth—no prayer ever fills a grumbling stomach—but in the ultimate sense, this is true. As living creatures, we need our Creator. God is, in fact, what we need. This is a glorious place for the Christian to come to, but the prerequisite, unfortunately, is pain. In the words of Elizabeth Elliot:

> When you are lonely, too much stillness is exactly the thing that seems to be laying waste your soul. Use that stillness to quiet your heart before God . . . Taken in the right spirit these very things will give us patient endurance; this in turn will develop a mature character, and a character of this sort produces a steady hope, a hope that will never disappoint us.[18]

It might sound strange to say this, but I wish that everyone could experience a season of loneliness. I know that every human feels lonely at times, but I am referring to an extended season of loneliness—the kind of season that stretches us, the kind that nobody wants. This is not my wish for the sake of the pain—I simply say it for the sake of the fruit. A season of loneliness can set the heart on fire, turning our focus toward Jesus. The truth is, marriage is not God's cure for loneliness—Jesus is. If we take this opportunity to chase after God, we will realize a striking reality: Our loneliness can draw us to Jesus.

Marriage is not God's cure for loneliness—Jesus is.

You Are Never Alone

In the book of 1 Kings, we come across a story about the prophet Elijah. His ministry on earth is nearly unmatched, filled to the brim with unthinkable miracles. But despite his powers and his connection with God, even Elijah was stricken with loneliness. On one particular night, God appeared to Elijah as he slept in a cave. He said to Elijah, "Go out and stand on the mountain before the Lord" (1 Kings 19:11 NASB). Then, Elijah witnessed a wind, an earthquake, a fire, and a whisper. While the Lord could not be found in the wind, the earthquake, or the fire, the Lord could be found in the still, small voice (1 Kings 19:12). The Lord then asked Elijah what he was doing in that cave, and his response revealed his loneliness:

> I have been very zealous for the Lord, the God of armies; for the sons of Israel have abandoned Your covenant, torn down Your altars, and killed Your prophets with the sword. And I alone am left. (1 Kings 19:14 NASB)

I alone am left, he said. Have you ever felt that way? I know I have! Perhaps all of your friends are already married. They are off raising children with no time to see you. Or, perhaps you're the oldest among your siblings—the one who was supposed to get married first—but now your siblings have skipped you in line. *I alone am left*, we say. This must have been how Elijah was feeling that night. He had done all the right things, his heart was the Lord's, and his circumstances were not to his liking. But even despite the earthquake, the fire, and hearing God's voice, Elijah was still fully convinced of his state of loneliness. He was fully convinced of his being alone. But God knew the truth of the matter. It was then that God shared the facts with Elijah, bringing an end to the cave-dweller's sorrows. God said:

Yet I have reserved seven thousand in Israel all whose knees have not bowed to Baal, and every mouth that has not kissed him. (1 Kings 19:18 NKJV)

While Elijah was convinced that he was alone, God had reserved seven thousand others who were just like him. They, too, loved the Lord and had not gone astray. The irony of that conversation is also not lost on me. Here, we have Elijah—a man who is fully assured of his terrible loneliness—and he is literally talking to someone. Even more so, that someone just happens to be God! This prophet had fallen for the lie that so often ensnares us. It is one of Satan's most common attacks. "You are alone," he whispers in our ears. "And no one is coming to join you."

But the Christian knows much better than that. There might be "seven thousand" singles who are in the same boat. The reality is, we are always with God and there are plenty of others, but our loneliness can keep us in caves. The good news is that we can use this loneliness to awaken our hearts, becoming fully aware of the love that we need.

As we learned from the story of Elijah:

With God, there will always be others.

TODAY'S CHALLENGE

Do you find yourself alone? Great! Close your door, turn on some worship music, and spend some time with the Lord. Enjoy Him. Be grateful for His love and character. But here's the thing: I don't want you to tell anyone about it. This is not a worship session we should see on social media. This is simply a meeting between you and God. Channel your loneliness as a means to connect with Him.

DAY FIFTEEN

YOUR FAITH

And without faith it is impossible to please him, for whoever would draw near
to God must believe that he exists and that he rewards those who seek him.
—HEBREWS 11:6

The man was named George Müller. He was born on September 27, 1805, in Kroppenstedt, Prussia (modern-day Germany). He was a wicked and worldly man. He was jailed at sixteen for both lying and robbery. After spending a full year in prison, the teenaged Müller was sent to a school in Nordhausen, where he continued his lifestyle of lewdness and sin. In his autobiography, Müller writes, "I felt no real remorse and cared nothing about the Word of God. I owned more than three hundred books, but no Bible . . . Nevertheless, the God whom I dishonored by my wicked behavior and unrepentant spirit had not given up on me."[9]

In the years that followed, George Müller eventually became a Christian. He would go on to be one of history's most faithful servants, living a life of simplicity and trusting the Lord. His testimony, to be frank, seems nearly impossible. He raised thousands of orphans throughout his lifetime, and all without drawing a salary! He meticulously documented God's answers to prayer because he

wanted to give God all the glory. Müller's journals eventually became his autobiography, which is still widely read today. On the first such occasion of answered prayer, Müller said this:

> On November 18, 1830, our money was reduced to about eight shillings (*roughly two days' wages*). When I was praying with my wife in the morning, I was led to ask the Lord for money. Four hours later, a sister said to me, "Do you want any money?" I replied, "I told the brethren when I gave up my salary that I would tell the Lord only about my wants." She said, "But He has told me to give you some money. About two weeks ago I asked Him what I should do for Him, and He told me to give you some money. Last Saturday the thought came again powerfully to my mind and has not left me since."[20]

This kind of provision would continue for a lifetime—and in increasing measure. God had given George Müller a heart for orphans, so while he started by raising one child, then two, then twelve, Müller eventually had several hundred children living under his care. For his entire life, Müller and his orphans were dependent on God. Somehow, someway, there was always enough money. Everyone's needs were met through prayer. Toward the end of his life, Müller wrote this:

> Every child of God is not called by the Lord to establish schools and orphan houses and to trust in the Lord for means for them. Yet, there is no reason why you may not experience, far more abundantly than we do now, His willingness to answer the prayers of His children.[21]

George Müller, through trial and error, had discovered the secret of faith. Our God is not dead, and our God is not distant. He is willing to help those who believe!

What Is Faith?

Throughout the course of the Bible, God repeatedly tells His people to have faith in His goodness. He calls His children to believe in His promises. It is clear that the practice of faith is of great importance to God, but this opens up a number of questions:

What is faith, really? How can we know when we have attained it? Why is it important for us to have faith? What is it about faith that stirs God's heart?

The writer of Hebrews described faith as "the certainty of things hoped for, a proof of things not seen" (Hebrews 11:1 NASB). Therefore, an obvious prerequisite for faith is not having the thing that you wish for. And then, just a few verses later, he said, "And without faith it is impossible to please him, for whoever would draw near to God must believe that he exists and that he rewards those who seek him" (Hebrews 11:6).

If you think about your favorite stories in Scripture, faith is almost always a common ingredient. Faith is the currency with which God transacts. In order to please God, we have to believe Him. We must believe that God is real, and we must believe that God offers rewards. God is not impressed by our talents, our bank accounts, or the praises of men, but His heart can be stirred by our faith. Notice how the book of Hebrews describes the saints:

Faith is the currency with which God transacts.

> By faith Noah, being warned by God concerning *events as yet unseen*, in reverent fear constructed an ark for the saving of his household. (Hebrews 11:7, emphasis added)

By faith Abraham obeyed when he was called to go out to a place that he was to receive as an inheritance. And he went out, *not knowing where he was going.* (Hebrews 11:8, emphasis added)

By faith Sarah herself received power to conceive, even when she was past the age, since *she considered him faithful* who had promised. (Hebrews 11:11, emphasis added)

The writer of Hebrews mentioned many other names, including Abel and Enoch, Isaac and Jacob, Joseph and Moses, and Rahab and Samson. He added in Jephthah, David, and Samuel as well. The names of these people are etched in history, remembered forever for their actions on earth. And what were their actions that are so worth remembering? They were men and women who expressed great faith. They believed in God and followed His Word.

There is an important aspect of faith that cannot be missed. Faith is always a matter of choice. I believe that this is why God is so moved by our faith, and this is why faith can make someone righteous. You might have heard it said, "If we *had* to love God, then that love would not be real." That is true. True love is—and must be—a choice. God does not want us to be robots whose love is not genuine. I believe it is the same when it comes to faith. For however long you walk this earth, you will always be faced with that choice. *What do you believe about God? Did Jesus actually die for your sins? Will you be a person of faith?* It is up to you to answer those questions. Only you can decide. But eventually, the time for choices and faith will be over. Once you leave this earth, your choice will be set, and having faith will no longer be possible. Have you realized that? We will not need faith once we cross into heaven. The gap will be closed. The disease abolished. If God tells us something, we will trust Him completely. If something is promised, we will know it will come. Today, we rely on faith, but then, we will know completely. As the apostle Paul said:

For now we see in a mirror dimly, but then face to face; now I know in part, but then I will know fully, just as I also have been fully known. (1 Corinthians 13:12 NASB)

FAITH IN ACTION

An act of faith always keeps the same pattern. There are four main phases to an act of faith, and they always appear in the same order: fear, faith, fulfillment, and fame.

First, a person will face insurmountable odds. Whether it be a financial situation or an opposing army, there is a natural circumstance that leads them to *fear*. Second, that person will choose the way of *faith*. They will believe in the thing that they hope God has told them. Third, God will come through and answer their prayers (*fulfillment*). And finally, the result of that fulfillment will increase God's *fame*. When someone is rescued from a personal peril, the Rescuer's story is magnified.

> *There are four main phases to an act of faith: fear, faith, fulfillment, and fame.*

Fear, faith, fulfillment, fame.

Let's look at an example in Scripture that follows this pattern, coming to us from 2 Chronicles 20. King Jehoshaphat of Judah was facing a dilemma, as the neighboring nations were threatening war. Knowing that Judah was far outnumbered and would likely be destroyed, Jehoshaphat called for a fast and cried out to God. As he stood in front of the people of Jerusalem, Jehoshaphat prayed these words to God:

> Now behold, the sons of Ammon, Moab, and Mount Seir, whom You did not allow Israel to invade when they came out of the land of Egypt (for they turned aside from them and did

not destroy them), see how they are rewarding us by coming to drive us out from Your possession which You have given us as an inheritance. Our God, will You not judge them? For we are powerless before this great multitude that is coming against us; nor do we know what to do, but our eyes are on You. (2 Chronicles 20:10–12 NASB)

Here we see a very human fear in the words of Jehoshaphat. He said that they were powerless against the might of their enemies. But then, he gives a faithful response. *Our eyes are on You.* Jehoshaphat knew that they were in trouble if God did not fight for them. The good news is, God had previously told them that He would fight for them, which gave the people of Judah a choice. Would they believe in the thing that God had promised? Would they take Him at His word? Speaking through the prophet, Jahaziel, God said this to the people of Judah:

Do not fear or be dismayed because of this great multitude, for the battle is not yours but God's. Tomorrow, go down against them. Behold, they will come up by the ascent of Ziz, and you will find them at the end of the valley in front of the wilderness of Jeruel. You need not fight in this battle; take your position, stand and watch the salvation of the Lord in your behalf, Judah and Jerusalem. (2 Chronicles 20:15–17 NASB)

God promised to fulfill their desires of faith. The people believed in their Rescuer, they cried out for help, and God was glad to provide them with rescue. In fact, what happened in their battle was quite bizarre. As the fighting commenced, God put the armies of Ammon, Moab, and Mount Seir in confusion, and they fought with each other! The armies of Israel just stood by and watched. They did not lift a sword. As is always the case with an act of faith, the God of Israel was exalted that day. As it says in the Scriptures:

> Every man of Judah and Jerusalem returned, with Jehoshaphat
> at their head, returning to Jerusalem with joy, for the Lord
> had helped them to rejoice over their enemies . . . And the
> dread of God was on all the kingdoms of the lands when they
> heard that the Lord had fought against the enemies of Israel.
> (2 Chronicles 20:27, 29 NASB)

Because of Jehoshaphat's faith—and God's fulfillment—all the nations of the world had witnessed God's strength. Fear, faith, fulfillment, fame. Evidently, God was not like the gods of their neighboring nations, those worthless idols of wood and stone.

God was living, and powerful, and ready to fight.

And He is fighting for you to this day.

TODAY'S CHALLENGE

Fill in the blanks.

What does the Bible say about God? What are your favorite parts of His character?

_____

_____

_____

_____

_____

_____

_____

Based on God's character, what can you know about your future?

_____

_____

_____

_____

Now believe it!

MIND

YOUR MONEY

The silver is Mine, and the gold is Mine.
—HAGGAI 2:8 NKJV

I worked as a financial advisor when I first moved to Nashville. During my time in finance, I was amazed at how singles would talk about money. Generally speaking, most singles I met with displayed little interest. There was rarely a plan or a strategy in place, and I saw very little long-term thinking. They cared more about vacations and that new item to purchase. The general sentiment I gathered was this: "I'll start caring about money once I'm married."

Now, I personally am a planner by nature, but even still, I could not grasp their logic in delaying their planning. Start caring about money when you're already married? But what if that day never comes? What then? Do you really think God will accept that excuse? Throughout the course of hundreds of meetings, I also noticed that singles used a similar verbiage. They used phrases like "my money" and "my resources" on a regular basis. This was coupled with *my* plans, *my* future, and *my* hopes and dreams. The problem is, the Bible says that all money is God's, not ours. Speaking through the prophet, Haggai, God plainly said, "The silver is Mine, and the gold is Mine" (Haggai 2:8 NKJV).

Could it be any clearer than that? God also emphasized this point in the book of Psalms, saying:

> For every beast of the forest is Mine, And the cattle on a thousand hills. I know all the birds of the mountains, And the wild beasts of the field are Mine. If I were hungry, I would not tell you; For the world is Mine, and all its fullness. (Psalm 50:10–12 NKJV)

The message of the Bible is clear and consistent. All the gold, all the silver, every bird, every beast, is God's. We own nothing. We rent everything. So then, let me ask you: How intentional are you in handling God's money? Are you waiting for marriage to be a good steward, or are you honoring God with His money right now?

—

We own nothing.

We rent everything.

—

If you were housesitting for someone, you would try to leave that house in a stellar condition. You would respect the owners' rules, clean up after yourself, and do everything possible to please them. You would do the same thing if you were dog-sitting, and you would certainly do this if you were babysitting. When someone entrusts you with their cherished possessions, the proper response is to handle them with care. You treat that possession even better than your own. You honor the giver by respecting the gift.

And we should handle God's money the same.

MISCONCEPTIONS ABOUT MONEY

Like many other topics that we find in the Bible, the subject of money has its own misconceptions. While an entire book could be written on this subject, we will focus our attention on three errors today. They are "God wants you to be rich," "Money does not buy happiness," and "Bring the tithe." Let's start with the first.

"God wants you to be rich." I have met some Christians who make this claim. They often use the riches of King David or King Solomon as proof of this fact. I have also heard people mention Jesus' tunic (John 19:23) as support for their stance about riches. "If Jesus had such a nice garment," they say, "then God must want the same thing for me!" In a way, I can understand how they could reach that conclusion. They are right in one sense. God does, in fact, want His children to be rich—just not in the way that they think.

While there is nothing wrong with treasures on earth, our true gifts await us in heaven. We are to set our minds on heavenly riches. Once a Christian is indwelt by the Holy Spirit, his appetite cannot help but change. As time goes on, the things of this world seem to decrease in value while the promises of heaven become more alluring. As human beings, we will always desire to possess good things, but our definition of good might change! Does God want us to be rich? Yes and no. He wants us to be rich in our faith.

"Money does not buy happiness." We have all heard this phrase. It is often taught by a well-meaning person with a heaven-focused perspective. This is good. But here is the thing that cannot be ignored: That statement is not always true. Money can *absolutely* buy you happiness. In fact, if money does not buy you happiness, then why does everyone chase it so much? It is *because* money buys happiness that we pay it so much attention.

If you think back to all of your favorite memories as a child—vacations, birthdays, concerts, and so on—you will notice that they all require the same thing: money. They all needed funding in order to happen. Truth be told, money can absolutely buy you happiness—often and predictably—but that happiness only stays for a moment. And that is the problem. This happiness runs out and must be replenished. On earth, this issue is often solved through monetary expenditure.

This is when our error kicks in. Instead of hoping in God and having treasures in heaven, we try to make ourselves happy on earth. It is this dependence on money—and chasing its pleasures—that can get us in trouble as Christians. As the apostle Paul once wrote:

> For the love of money is a root of all kinds of evils. It is through this craving that some have wandered away from the faith and pierced themselves with many pangs. (1 Timothy 6:10)

Make no mistake: Money does buy happiness—but it does not buy salvation. It does not meet your need to be one with your Maker. If you decide to purchase your joy with money, it will become a never-ending enterprise. It will also do nothing to pay for your sin. Like carrying a bucket with a hole in the bottom, that kind of happiness will always escape you. Happiness from money is real, but fleeting. It is rented, not owned. But our joy in the Lord is forever.

MISQUOTING MALACHI

Before we end our discussion on money, I think it is important for us to discuss one last misconception. Let's now talk about tithing, and how the Christian should give to church and charity.

"Bring the tithe," the pastor says. This is a very common phrase in churches today. As a result, many people falsely believe that this is a black-and-white formula—and the biblical prescription for giving. It is not. This *was* the formula for giving in Old Testament Israel, but it does not apply to us today.

In the Mosaic Law, God commanded the people of Israel to donate a tithe. To "tithe" something meant to "give one-tenth of." The tribe of Levi—often referred to as the Levites—were in charge of the priestly duties in Israel. They were the ones who received this tithe. These priests offered animal sacrifices and prayers to the Lord, which prevented them from earning a living through farming and trading. Therefore, the Levites needed economic support to put food on the table. This is why God commanded the Israelites to bring the tithe—to help the Levites feed themselves. In that sense, the Old Testament practice of tithing is quite similar to our taxes today. The Levites—like our government officials—provided a service with no monetary output. In other words, they had to meet their needs through a form of taxation.

It should also be noted that there were actually *three* tithes, not just one, that were imposed on Old Testament Israel. The Israelites were required to give ten percent to the Levites (Numbers 18:21–24), another ten percent to the feasts and festivals (Deuteronomy 14:22–27), and then, on every third year, yet another ten percent to the poor and needy (Deuteronomy 14:28–29). There was, effectively speaking, a *twenty-three* percent tithe written into their law book. I have yet to meet a Christian who adheres to this number.

There were actually three tithes, not just one, that were imposed on Old Testament Israel.

It is within this context that we should think about tithing. The tithe was a commandment for Old Testament Israel—a tax, a function of society—and it is no longer applicable today. Nevertheless, the practice of tithing is still taught in our churches. "Bring the tithe," the pastors say, "and see how God will bless you." Oftentimes, these well-meaning pastors will reference Malachi 3:10 in order to justify this teaching. That verse says this:

> "Bring the whole tithe into the storehouse, so that there may be food in My house, and put Me to the test now in this," says the LORD of armies, "if I do not open for you the windows of heaven and pour out for you a blessing until it overflows." (Malachi 3:10 NASB)

That sounds great. Does it not? God will pour out His blessings until they overflow? Not to mention, God gives us permission to actually test Him?

No. Wrong.

God is not giving you permission to test Him with tithing—not unless you are an Old Testament Jew. Again, the practice of tithing was a specific command—for a specific nation, at a specific time— and so was this promise in Malachi. In fact, it is simply by putting this verse in the proper context that this truth will make itself plain.

In Malachi 3:9 (just one verse earlier), God had said this to the Israelites, "You are under a curse—your whole nation—because you are robbing me" (Malachi 3:9 NIV). This curse is in reference to Deuteronomy 28:15–68, where God laid out dozens of punishments that He would inflict on disobedience. God promised the curses of famine (v. 18), drought (v. 24), stolen produce (v. 33), destructive insects (vv. 38–39), enemy oppression (v. 48), and deadly plagues (v. 59). And then, when the Israelites had failed to bring the tithe, God literally came through on His promises. He cursed them with all of those horrible things (no rain, no crops, bad bugs, etc.).

So then, let me ask you this: If you are willing to accept God's blessing (Malachi 3:10), are you equally willing to accept God's curse (Malachi 3:9)? It is both, or neither. You cannot have it both ways. Or, asked in a different way: Do you honestly believe that your lack of giving will cause a drought in America? If you refuse to tithe, should we expect a famine? Of course not. God is speaking to Israel in Malachi 3, not a twenty-first-century Christian.

At this point, you might be asking yourself, "Well, if we are not supposed to bring the tithe, then how are we supposed to give? What is the protocol for Christians like me?" The truth of the matter is, you and I reflect God in a different way. Our new covenant giving is actually better than the out-of-date blessing in Malachi. God does not give us His riches to make us a spectacle; He gives them so we can be generous. The key passage on that comes from 2 Corinthians 9, where Paul writes:

> Remember this: Whoever sows sparingly will also reap sparingly, and whoever sows generously will also reap generously. Each of you should give what you have decided in your heart to give, not reluctantly or under compulsion for God loves a cheerful giver. (2 Corinthians 9:6–7 NIV)

The modern-day Christian gives freely and joyfully. The New Testament giver only does so by choice. There *is* no tithe for the Christian today. We give to God because we love Him, not because we are commanded to. Is it still good for us to give to the church? Of course! It is in God's nature to be charitable to others. But, it is for our own spiritual growth—not because of commands or compulsions—that God asks us to give from our resources. God gives us His money so we can give it to others. God blesses us so that we, too, can bless. Paul continued in his letter to the Corinthians:

—

You will be enriched in every way so that you can be generous on every occasion.

—2 CORINTHIANS 9:11 NIV

—

> And God is able to bless you abundantly, so that in all things at all times, having all that you need, you will abound in every good work . . . You will be enriched in every way so that you can be generous on every occasion, and through us your generosity will result in thanksgiving to God. (2 Corinthians 9:8, 11 NIV)

Why does God give His children money? So that they can give it away freely and generate thanksgiving. In the Old Testament era, Israel received God's blessing by enriching themselves, thus making them the envy of neighboring nations. In the new covenant era, however, the Christian receives God's resources and spreads them to others—and he does so voluntarily, at that. The more that we give, the more praise God gets. It was Jesus Himself who said, "It is more blessed to give than to receive" (Acts 20:35).

Old Testament believers were bound to a code, but new covenant believers just give from the heart. We enjoy a joyous, selfless, free-spirited generosity, and it resembles the character of Jesus. This type of giving can make us slippery to Satan, further breaking our ties to the material world. While we might possess money, it does not possess us, and that is what Jesus intended.

On the subject of money, remember this truth:

When your silver and gold are God's, your heart will be God's as well.

TODAY'S CHALLENGE

Partake in a radical, spontaneous act of giving.
Make someone's day!

You can give to a person on the corner, a cause that you believe in, or even your church. You can give a monetary gift, or material goods. Just be generous! And then, once you have given this generous gift, experience the thanksgiving that all giving brings.

A closing prayer:
"Thank You, Father, for giving me the
means to share love with this person."

DAY SEVENTEEN

YOUR HOPES
AND DREAMS

You do not know what will happen tomorrow . . . Instead you ought
to say, "If the Lord wills, we shall live and do this or that."
—JAMES 4:14, 15 NKJV

I could not believe what I was reading. It was the most arrogant
introduction I had ever seen. *Did he really just say that?* I thought.

The book was *Secrets of a Prayer Warrior*, and it was written
by Derek Prince. Prince had long since passed by the time of my
reading, but I was looking for some guidance on prayer. And then, I
came to his introduction.

"I get what I pray for," he says on page one.[22]

I get what I pray for? Who does this guy think he is?

Come to find out, Derek Prince did get what he prayed for, early
and often, and the same can be said of you and me. In the next few
pages, I am going to teach you why your prayers are not being answered, and I will give you a guaranteed tactic to fix it.

FADING PLEASURES

When considering the human condition, one thing cannot be denied: We human beings have desires. We want things. In fact, we want the best that this world has to offer. We scratch and claw—or passively wait—for better houses, higher incomes, or more attractive partners. Some of us even attain these things, but their state of grandeur never seems to remain. For some reason, their beauty and newness cannot be sustained. To quote C. S. Lewis:

> The longings which arise in us when we first fall in love, or first think of some foreign country, or first take up some subject that excites us, are longings which no marriage, no travel, no learning, can really satisfy. I am not now speaking of what would be ordinarily called unsuccessful marriages, or holidays, or learned careers. I am speaking of the best possible ones. There was something we grasped at, in that first moment of longing, which just fades away in the reality. I think everyone knows what I mean.[23]

Our hopes and dreams run on a closed loop. Round and round and round they go. From inception to planning to fulfillment to boredom, our dreams can never sustain us. They simply are a race that cannot be won, but many people try for a lifetime.

WHY HOPES AND DREAMS DO NOT COME TRUE

What are you dreaming about these days? I am sure there is something. Is it a new living situation? A new profession? Finding a spouse? Whatever it may be, the fact that you are still "dreaming" about it means your desires have not been fulfilled. Your hopes have yet to align with reality. I can certainly understand how that feels.

There are three possible reasons why our dreams do not happen: God's timing, our pride, or our ignorance. Let's address each of them now, in turn.

First, for *God's timing*. This is the most straightforward reason why our dreams do not manifest. You might be on the exact right path that God wants you to be, but He will deliver the blessing at a later date. In situations like that, we are called to a life of praying, trusting, and waiting on God. He will likely have some lessons for us along the way. While this explanation does not lift the pains of waiting, we can have hope it is worth it in the end. As it says in the book of Proverbs, "Hope deferred makes the heart sick, but a desire fulfilled is a tree of life" (Proverbs 13:12).

Second, *our pride* can prevent our prayers from being answered. Pride can certainly prevent us from receiving God's blessings. (We discussed this in detail on Day Eleven.) We see an example of this in the story of Naaman, who nearly forfeited a miracle because of dumb expectations. As the Bible says, Naaman was a "commander of the army of the king of Aram . . . a valiant soldier, but he had leprosy" (2 Kings 5:1 NIV). When Naaman sought out a remedy to heal his leprosy, he traveled to Israel in search of an answer. He eventually found the prophet Elisha, who was known for performing such miracles. Naaman firmly believed that he was able to heal him.

Once Naaman had come to the house of Elisha, he stood at the door and presented his case. But Elisha—who seemed completely disinterested in playing the host—would not even give him an audience. Instead, he sent a servant to give him a message. The servant said, "Go, wash yourself seven times in the Jordan, and your flesh will be

Hope deferred makes the heart sick, but a desire fulfilled is a tree of life.

—PROVERBS 13:12

restored and you will be cleansed" (2 Kings 5:10 NIV). But Naaman did not like that answer. Here is what happened next:

> But Naaman went away angry and said, "I thought that he would surely come out to me and stand and call on the name of the Lord his God, wave his hand over the spot and cure me of my leprosy. Are not Abana and Pharpar, the rivers of Damascus, better than all the waters of Israel? Couldn't I wash in them and be cleansed?" So he turned and went off in a rage. (2 Kings 5:11–12 NASB)

The miracle was not big enough in the eyes of Naaman. Elisha had wrecked his plans, offered something less flashy, and Naaman stormed off like a child. I wonder how often we do the same thing. How often does God offer us something that we refuse to accept? How often are we deeming God's gifts too boring or mundane? Luckily for Naaman, his servants maintained a heart of humility. As he stormed away from Elisha, his servants stopped him and said:

> My father, if the prophet had told you to do some great thing, would you not have done it? How much more, then, when he tells you, "Wash and be cleansed"! (2 Kings 5:13 NIV)

Because of their challenge, Naaman eventually went to the Jordan. He washed himself seven times—as unspectacular as that may sound—and his leprosy was cured forever. In fact, the Bible says that his skin became like that of a young boy (2 Kings 5:14 NIV). He received a spectacular gift through some ordinary means. The moral of this story is simple: Our pride can prevent us from receiving God's gifts. One act of obedience can change that fact.

And finally, the third reason why our dreams do not come true is because of *our ignorance*—ignorance of the reason why God answers prayer. Have you ever asked *why* God might give you your desires? Have you ever stopped to consider His motivation? Well, if you look to the Bible, you will find a common theme. The answer might even surprise you.

In our modern-day, American-dream-infused Christianity, we are taught to believe that God loves to bless us. To be more specific, we are taught to believe that God likes what we like. As if God is the genie in our magical bottles, we are told to pray boldly and "believe for the miracle." And then, we cherry-pick Scripture. We lie to ourselves. We read things into the Bible that are not actually there. We claim that our "wants" are really God's "promises."

While God might still give us the things we desire, His ultimate aim is much higher than that. This is why so many of our prayers will never be answered—because we are ignorant of God's true intentions for our lives. God will not answer a prayer that is selfish in nature. The apostle James said this on the subject of prayer:

> You do not have because you do not ask. You ask and do not receive, because you ask with the wrong motives, so that you may spend what you request on your pleasures . . . Or do you think that the Scripture says to no purpose, "He jealously desires the Spirit whom He has made to dwell in us"? (James 4:2–3, 5 NASB)

You have not because you ask not. Upon hearing this teaching, what is the first thing that most of us do in response? We ask! We boldly approach God and present our requests. But then, when our prayers go unanswered, we wonder if God is not listening to us. Why does this happen? What are we doing wrong? While God's answer might be delayed due to timing or pride, James presents another reason that is perfectly viable. Our prayers are not answered because of our ignorance. We are blind to the mind and heart of our Father.

Why would a loving God ever give us the career, house, or spouse of our dreams if He knew they would pull us away from Him? As James wrote in his letter, God has put the Holy Spirit in us, and He jealously desires the love of that Spirit. God only answers the prayers that coincide with that truth.

GOD'S DREAM FOR US

God wants to fulfill our wildest dreams. He does. The problem is, when most of us read "our wildest dreams," we think of a dream for this lifetime. We think of houses, spouses, health, and wealth. But God has a different dream for us. He is shifting our minds to think outside this world.

The key to answered prayer, therefore, is to let God inform your desires. The first thing to be done in achieving this end is to rid yourself of all expectations. This decision might be simple, but it is not easy. It means letting go of everything you've ever dreamed of—the family, the money, the beaches, the comforts, and everything else that you have on your vision board. But then, once you allow God's dreams to become your own, just see what happens next. You will progressively adopt the character of Jesus, you will become increasingly useful in the hand of the Lord, and—wouldn't you know it—your prayers will start being answered! Now that your prayers are aligned with God's will, the answers will come with abandon. In a sense, they are really God's prayers being passed through your lips. As Elisabeth Elliott once observed:

> I realized that the deepest spiritual lessons are not learned by His letting us have our way in the end, but by His making us wait, bearing with us in love and patience until we are able honestly to pray what He taught His disciples to pray: Thy will be done.[24]

God is only interested in fulfilling our dreams if those dreams are aligned with His will. He is, after all, a jealous God (Exodus 34:14) who continually guides our steps (Proverbs 19:21). Once the Christian starts dreaming God's dreams, he will pray God's prayers, and his prayers will be answered. *Father, make Your dreams my dreams.* If you empty yourself and pray that prayer, you can know that your dreams will be accomplished. The challenge, of course, is changing our desires to be aligned with the Lord. Our level of surrender will only rise to our trust. It is for this reason that we don't pray for God's will—we simply do not trust in His goodness.

Your God wants you to prosper, and He wants you to have fruit, but He is in charge of your future. He is the One who directs your steps. Therefore, you can be stiff and stubborn and not turn to God, or you can humble yourself and start praying God's will. The choice is yours. If God tells you to wash in the Jordan, please go. If He tells you to wait for your marriage, please wait.

By aligning with God, your future is assured. And then, you will get what you pray for.

—

God is only interested in fulfilling our dreams if those dreams are aligned with His will.

—

Today's Challenge

Answer these questions about hopes and dreams:

1) What is your biggest dream/desire?

_____

_____

_____

_____

2) How could God, the Lover of your soul, be using this dream to draw you to Him?

_____

_____

_____

_____

3) How could Satan, the enemy of your soul, be using this dream to pull you from God?

_____

_____

_____

_____

DAY EIGHTEEN

YOUR MUSIC
AND MEDIA

Finally, brothers and sisters, whatever is true, whatever is noble, whatever
is right, whatever is pure, whatever is lovely, whatever is admirable—if
anything is excellent or praiseworthy—think about such things.
—PHILIPPIANS 4:8 NIV

Our God is an artist, of that I am sure. We witness His brilliance at the time of a sunset, and we witness His heart when a bird lifts its song. Whether we're pondering the differences of the seasons, the rings of Saturn, or the seventeen thousand different species of butterflies, the universe possesses an impossible diversity—and for seemingly no distinct reason![25] The world would still spin if the sky were gray, but the Artist has decided that it should be blue. Likewise, when God was making His flying creatures, He could have made one variation and just called it "bird." But He didn't do that. Instead, God made eagles and falcons and pigeons and doves. He made thousands and thousands and thousands of birds.

This consistent pattern of creativity tells us something about God's character. Our God is expressive and playful in nature. He is, in a word, artistic. Where else would we humans have gotten that from? There is something unique about art that only God—and His imagers, by extension—can display. If we are being honest, artwork truly has no external utility. It is completely different from other inventions. Art does not drive a nail into a piece of wood, nor can it drive a person to the grocery store. A beaver does not build his dam with art. And yet, we know that art has an obvious purpose—it helps us experience beauty. Our music and artwork are created for enjoyment, but they also can lead to our doom.

THE DANGERS OF MEDIA

The human mind is truly quite malleable, and the human heart is desperate to belong. As a result of this dangerous mix, we need to be very aware of the things we consume. If we are not careful, we might end up surrounded by negative influences, thus corrupting our character as time goes by. Therefore, we must be militant about the media we allow in our lives.

The ease with which we live today is remarkable. Mankind has never been more comforted, more entertained, and frankly, less alive. Between our washing machines, air conditioning, and the bevy of apps that can bring us our food, the modern-day man lives like kings of old. While we claim to be busier than ever—and this certainly carries some truth—we still have more downtime than we know what to do with. How else can we describe our hours of scrolling?

—

Mankind has never been more comforted, more entertained, and less alive.

—

And how do we typically fill this time? *Consumption.* A virtual feast of endless consumption. We stream movies, listen to podcasts, and scroll social media at all hours of the day. We have become dopamine-chasing, glazed-eyed zombies, hunting likes and comments like an addict seeks substances. It was Ed Cole who once said, "The greatest addiction in America is not marijuana, cocaine, or pills. It is television."[26] While his words still hold some merit today (they were published in 2001), I would slightly revise them for the modern-day reader. The truth is, the greatest addiction in America today is the rectangle that lives in our pockets. That's right, our cell phones. With its endless applications, social media outlets, and, yes, even television on-demand, the cell phone is the greatest addiction in America—and it poses a threat to our pursuit of godliness.

Knowing that a sinful man will always chase comfort, Satan uses our media to pull us from God. As long as we are occupied by mindless things, our hearts will be distracted from the One we desire. Our media can even distract us from our nature as humans, causing us to lose sight of our status as artists. Let me ask you, when was the last time you wrote a poem? When was the last time you sang a song? How about painting a picture? Sanding a deck? Building a house? Planting a garden? We are constantly consuming but rarely creating. Sure, we might post a quick video on social media, but it's irrelevant by daybreak tomorrow. I am talking about something that really lasts, something that makes you think, sweat, and dream.

We lose sight of the artist in us because of distractions, with our media being chief among them. This should never be the case when describing God's imagers. We are made in His image and reflect His nature, which means we are capable of beauty.

The Christian and Media

It is often said that we are the sum of our five closest friends. I am sure you have heard this expression before. The moral of this saying, of course, is to surround yourself with the right kind of friends. We become just like the people we surround ourselves with. This is a common phrase, and its wisdom is sound, but I would like to offer my personal amendment. Here is how I would change this "five-person" adage:

We are not the sum of our five closest friends. We are actually the sum of our five biggest inputs. What do I mean by this? Well, in our highly virtual, isolationist world, our five biggest influences are not always friends. They are not always the people that we see every day. While this might sound odd to hear, let's just run some quick math to see if it's true. Tell me, in the last week, how many hours did you spend on social media? How many movies or shows did you stream online? How many podcasts or playlists were blared through your headphones? And then, by comparison:

How many hours did you spend with your five closest friends?

Now can you see what I mean?

We are actually the sum of our five biggest inputs. This means that the books we read matter, the shows we watch matter, and the posts that our algorithm feeds us all matter. So then, the natural question must follow: What kind of music and media are we allowing to influence us? How we answer this question will dictate our character. For example, let's say that you are caught up in a hit television series—with either death, dragons, and medieval orgies, or cowboys, ranches, and bloody revenge. All of a sudden, you find yourself cussing more often and thinking about sex. You are more anxious and vengeful. If your mind is a sponge, and you feed it these inputs, is it really a wonder if your brain starts to crave them? Can you really be shocked if you parrot those characters?

> *We are not the sum of our five closest friends. We are actually the sum of our five biggest inputs.*

It is just the same with social media, and it is just the same when it comes to music. Our choice of music can shape our world. In a quote widely attributed to Blaise Pascal, he noted, "It's not those who write the laws that have the greatest impact on society. It's those who write the songs."[27]

We become like the people that we congregate with. This is true. But we also become like the things we consume. The host of your favorite podcast has just as much influence as a friend. They have your attention for hours at a time. Their thoughts are shaping your own. You wouldn't be lewd or lazy about picking your friends, so why do so when picking your media? Remember, we eventually become like the things we consume. In that vein, the apostle Paul issued this warning to the Christians in Philippi:

> Finally, brothers and sisters, whatever is true, whatever is noble, whatever is right, whatever is pure, whatever is lovely, whatever is admirable—if anything is excellent or praiseworthy—think about such things. (Philippians 4:8 NIV)

In light of this counsel, the intentional Christian consumes with a purpose. We are mindful of what we allow in our hearts. On a personal level, I myself have had to cut out a few of my favorite podcasts and television shows for this reason. Though I enjoyed the content in one sense, there was also a part of me that just did not feel right. I noticed that the television show made me prideful, and the radio show made me stressed. Plus, both of these programs took the Lord's name in vain, and each time I heard that, I cringed. Needless to say, these shows were not "excellent or praiseworthy" in the eyes of the Lord, and they were draining the joy from my life. While they were originally fun and easy to consume, I did not like their long-term effects, so they had to go.

Perhaps there are some things in your life that might need to be cut. Maybe that true-crime podcast is not really serving you. Maybe reality television does not bring out your best. Tell me: Would you like to become a petty, worldly, dramatic gossip like the ones that we see on television? Of course not. And yet, some so-called "Bible studies" schedule parties just to watch this stuff. It is wine and gossip under the guise of piety. But the Bible suggests a different approach.

TRY SOMETHING NEW

As we conclude our thoughts about music and media, I think it is also worthwhile to discuss one final thing. Knowing that we are created in God's image, I think it is important for us to explore that image. (I am specifically referring to the world of art.) This "artsy" crusade can take any number of forms. Perhaps you buy a ticket to an art museum. Maybe you attend a show at your local symphony. Maybe you go to a play or a Broadway musical. There are so many forms of art to enjoy, and each of them offers unique blessings. But what do they all have in common? They are ways we reflect the image of God. They are windows through which we see Jesus.

As Paul says in his epistle, "For by Him all things were created that are in heaven and that are on earth, visible and invisible, whether thrones or dominions or principalities or powers. All things were created through Him and for Him" (Colossians 1:16 NKJV).

We Christians are artists. We are playful, joyful, beautiful artists. We mirror our music and media.

TODAY'S CHALLENGE

Do a media audit.

Make an honest assessment of the music, books, podcasts, and shows that you consume on a regular basis. (These are, after all, the inputs that are shaping your life.) Are your choices of media pleasing to God, or are they really just pleasing your flesh?

After your audit is complete, be sure to *replace* any bad inputs with things that are good. This is key. You must replace the old inputs with things that are positive. This means you might be deleting some playlists and creating some more. For example, if you want to stop listening to that rap music from high school, then replace it with a playlist of worship music instead. If you want to stop scrolling on social media, then pick a book (or a project) that can be your new pastime.

YOUR SPEECH

In the multitude of words sin is not lacking,
but he who restrains his lips is wise.
—PROVERBS 10:19 NKJV

This man had been born for war. He was the general of a newly formed army, and he was facing an impossible task. Some historians believe it was the most audacious mission in military history, and yet, he stood resolute. Their enemy was the greatest force the world had ever known, and it carried out the will of a tyrant. Though he knew that his troops were outgunned and outmanned, he believed he had the favor of Providence.

There was, however, one thing that greatly troubled this man. As he looked upon his scattered battalions, he noticed something that greatly displeased him. A vile practice had spread among his men, polluting their ranks at alarming speed. This act was so despicable—so damning, in fact—that he felt it could threaten their victory. Providence would surely detest such a thing.

And so, the general sat down and penned his order. He would put an end to this practice and salvage their victory. He wrote:

The General is sorry to be informed that the foolish, and wicked practice, of profane cursing and swearing (a Vice heretofore little known in an American Army) is growing into fashion; he hopes the officers will, by example, as well as influence, endeavour to check it, and that both they, and the men will reflect, that we can have little hopes of the blessing of Heaven on our Arms, if we insult it by our impiety, and folly; added to this, it is a vice so mean and low, without any temptation, that every man of sense, and character, detests and despises it.[28]

His order was dispersed. The general had spoken. He could not allow such small, ugly, putrid behavior to infect the soul of his nation. If he and his men were to conquer their giants, their first step was to conquer their tongues.

That letter was drafted on August 3, 1776.

Its author was General George Washington.

—

It is a vice so mean and low, without any temptation, that every man of sense, and character, detests and despises it.

— GEORGE WASHINGTON

—

THE UNTAMABLE BEAST

The tongue is a powerful tool. It has the ability to heal past wounds and mend broken hearts. When they are used correctly, our words have the power to bless, build up, and motivate others to be their best selves. There is, however, a much uglier side to the human tongue. Very few of us follow the General's orders. It is this fallen, sinful side of our speech that the Bible so often addresses. The Bible describes the tongue as dirty, wretched, and even untamable. As the apostle James once wrote:

And the tongue is a fire, a world of unrighteousness. The tongue is set among our members, staining the whole body, setting on fire the entire course of life, and set on fire by hell. For every kind of beast and bird, of reptile and sea creature, can be tamed and has been tamed by mankind, but no human being can tame the tongue. It is a restless evil, full of deadly poison. With it we bless our Lord and Father, and with it we curse people who are made in the likeness of God. (James 3:6–9)

George Washington thought swearing was wicked and foolish. "Every man of sense despises it," he said. James believed that the tongue was a restless, evil, deadly poison. An untamed tongue reveals the depth of our sinfulness. As the Bible warns us again and again:

A worthless person, a wicked man, is one who walks with a perverse mouth. (Proverbs 6:12 NASB)

Those who guard their lips preserve their lives, but those who speak rashly will come to ruin. (Proverbs 13:3 NIV)

If you claim to be religious but don't control your tongue, you are fooling yourself, and your religion is worthless. (James 1:26 NLT)

Even Jesus Himself said:

I tell you, on the day of judgment people will give account for every careless word they speak, for by your words you will be justified, and by your words you will be condemned. (Matthew 12:36–37)

So then, how are we called to tame our tongues? What things should we allow to escape our lips? Well, the good news is, the Bible has plenty to say there as well.

WORDS OF HEALING

When issuing a prescription on taming the tongue, we first must remember its nature. Our tongue is a child, an infant, a horse in the wild that has yet to be broken. The intentional Christian brings a bit to that horse. Just like we would with a newborn child, we must tell our tongues what is right and wrong. We must guide our tongues to a state of maturity. Paul did this very thing with his children of the faith, writing this to the Christians at Philippi:

> Do all things without grumbling or disputing, that you may be blameless and innocent, children of God without blemish in the midst of a crooked and twisted generation, among whom you shine as lights in the world. (Philippians 2:14–15)

Do all things without grumbling. Here Paul emphasizes the importance of taming the tongue. By doing this, he claimed, the Philippians would become blameless, innocent children of God. He also added this in his letter to Titus:

> Likewise urge the young men to be sensible; in all things show yourself to be an example of good deeds, with purity in doctrine, dignified, sound in speech which is beyond reproach, so that the opponent will be put to shame, having nothing bad to say about us. (Titus 2:6–8 NASB)

Paul knew that our speech can make us look different. Our tongues can distinguish us Christians from the rest of the crowd. When we do not grumble or complain—especially when our life is impossibly difficult—then we shine as a light to the people around us. And

The well-trained tongue is a balm to the hurting.

then, when our acquaintances find themselves in tough situations, they remember the conduct we displayed. They remember the purity, the dignity, the soundness of speech, and the general peace in "that Christian from work." Then, they reach out for help in search of our secret, and we are able to share the gospel. By not grumbling, complaining, or cursing those around us, we leave space for good words to come in and heal. The well-trained tongue is a balm to the hurting.

QUIET YOURSELF BEFORE THE LORD

With time and diligence, the tongue can eventually be put in its place. While this job of "taming" is never fully completed, a notable shift will be seen in the Christian. The cursing and swearing will leave their vocabulary. There is, however, a place that many of us have started to err. This error is especially common in charismatic circles.

In our closeness, proximity, and desire for God, our approach to prayer can sometimes be flippant. Sometimes, the immature Christian grows too casual in prayer, casting all awe and reverence aside. This often expresses itself in a kind of foot-stomping, finger-pointing, "wrestling-with-God" type of prayer. These prayers are often encouraged by charismatic pastors, saying things like, "God can take it!" and, "Come as you are!" Yes, the Bible does tell us to be honest with God, and God can obviously handle anything that we say, but that does not mean that these prayers are godly—and it does not mean that these prayers are answered. If you are a foot-stomping, finger-pointing, "wrestles-with-God" kind of person, I would kindly encourage you to reflect on Day Eight (Your Church). Remember: There are two things necessary for a balanced faith: the fear of the Lord and the comfort of the Holy Spirit. The person who yells at the Lord lacks this fear, and God does not answer prayers on account of their volume. Our fear of the Lord must be equal to—and work in tandem with—our comfort in Him, and it can often be seen in our speech. As King Solomon once wrote:

> Do not be quick with your mouth or impulsive in thought to bring up a matter in the presence of God. For God is in heaven and you are on the earth; therefore let your words be few. (Ecclesiastes 5:2 NASB)

Fear and comfort; speech and silence. The Christian must exercise both. Like the humbled Job before our God, we too can honestly say, "Behold, I am insignificant; what can I say in response to You? I put my hand on my mouth" (Job 40:4 NASB).

The tongue can be a powerful thing, and we have been called to corral it. No matter what trial or situation we may be faced with—whether it be a failed relationship, a horrible illness, or an army of redcoats—God blesses the man who has tamed his tongue. It is not easy, it is not natural, but it is our duty to guard it.

We can bless and heal with the fruit of our words.

All our speech must be pleasing to Providence.

Today's Challenge

Reflect on your conversations and prayers from this past week. How did they go? Were your words quick and impulsive, or were they measured and wise? What did you do well? What could you have done differently?

YOUR SILENCE

For God alone, O my soul, wait in silence, for my hope is from him.
—PSALM 62:5

My dad grew up in the Pacific Northwest. I still have family members living on much of the West Coast. From Seattle to Eugene, from San Diego to Salem, you'll find Wheatleys all up and down the Interstate 5.

On one particular morning, I had woken up in Eugene, Oregon. I was spending some time at my grandparents' house. They had planned a large family gathering for the following week, and I was tasked with picking up my cousin in Portland. All that was needed was a ninety-minute drive, but that drive would be truly transformative.

When I set out that morning, I really had no plans for a "life-changing" journey. Truth be told, I was really just struck by the scenery I saw. If you have ever been to Oregon in the summertime, you know what I mean. There was not a cloud in the sky that day, and the flowers and trees were serene. It was beautiful.

When I was eventually tempted to turn on some music, I paused. I decided against it. I figured the tunes could wait for another five minutes. The landscape was just too spectacular to ignore. And then, five minutes became ten. Ten minutes became twenty. Twenty minutes became—as I'm sure you can guess—the entire ninety minutes to Portland. I drove 110 miles in absolute silence. There was no podcast or playlist or person to talk to. It was just me and the Oregon countryside.

And it was magical.

My soul was singing when I arrived in Portland. I was calm, refreshed, and filled with joy. I had no idea how our silence could affect us, nor did I understand its effects on our faith.

A Noisy World

We have so much going on these days. Perhaps more than any time in history, our minds are more overwhelmed than ever before. We have texts, we have chats, we have posts, we have pings. The onslaught of noises is truly unending. I have noticed this trend in my own life, as well—there is constantly noise in my eardrums.

Jazz music when I am cooking dinner.

Sermons when I am in the car.

Podcasts when I am at the gym.

The noise just never ends.

While our technologies make learning far more accessible, there is also a tradeoff that comes with this learning. It is very "American" of us to want to improve, achieve, and succeed in our callings. There is nothing wrong with a good day's work, but this drive to accomplish does cause much of our noise. Yes, we are learning. Yes, we are achieving. But at what cost? In 2 Timothy 3, Paul warns us that some well-meaning believers are "always learning but never able to come to a knowledge of the truth" (2 Timothy 3:7 NIV). And that is the trap—we can fall in love with our "learning."

There comes a point in time where more information is not helpful. You do not need a new teacher, preacher, mentor, or guide. If you already have the truth at your disposal, you might just need some room to breathe. Deep thoughts require time and space. It is only through reflection and silence that truth can take root.

I am reminded of a scene in one of my favorite novels. In Alexandre Dumas' *The Count of Monte Cristo*, the young Edmond Dantès has been wrongly accused. After being thrown into prison, Edmond burrows his way to the neighboring cell, eventually striking up a friendship with the old man next door. The man's name is Abbe Faria, and he is immeasurably and impossibly wise. He speaks over a dozen languages, he wields every weapon with mastery, he can read, write, and invent things at will, and he knows every cuisine and custom. Naturally, Edmond is amazed by the mind of Abbe Faria despite his clear disadvantage as a prisoner. This leads Edmond to ask him:

> I was reflecting, in the first place, upon the enormous degree
> of intelligence and ability you must have employed to reach
> the high perfection to which you have attained—if you thus
> surpass all mankind while but a prisoner, what would you not
> have accomplished free?[29]

Surely, if the abbe had served all those years as a priest, professor, or politician, then his mind could have taken him to much greater heights. Perhaps he would have been rich, powerful, and had men bow at his feet! But then, the abbe responds in an unexpected way. *What would he have accomplished if he were a free man?*

> Possibly nothing at all—the overflow of my brain would prob-
> ably in a state of freedom have evaporated in a thousand follies.
> It needs trouble and difficulty and danger to hollow out various
> mysteries and hidden mines of human intelligence. Pressure is
> required, you know, to ignite powder; captivity has collected
> into one single focus all the floating faculties of my mind.[30]

It was pressure that afforded Faria his brilliance. Because of the difficulty of his captivity—because of those years of silence that were thrust upon him—he was able to focus and work on his mind. He was a prisoner. He had no distractions. If he had been a priest or professor or politician, then the "follies" of life might have gotten in the way. The same can be said of Dietrich Bonhoeffer, who wrote so prolifically from prison that we've literally made a book from it. Bonhoeffer's *Letters and Papers from Prison* was published posthumously by his friend and biographer, Eberhard Bethge.[31]

That is exactly what we are missing today. Time. Space. *Silence.* We are constantly distracted with mindless nonsense. We scroll social media. We throw on a movie. We listen to a podcast. We listen to a playlist of our favorite songs.

And we never leave room just to think.

HEARING THE WHISPERS

In our hustle and bustle and constant noise, we slowly slip away from our God. We drown Him out with noisier things. We miss out on the Voice who speaks in a whisper.

I have met many people who struggle with faith. They say that they do not feel or sense God in their everyday lives. The idea of connecting with Him, being led by Him, and ultimately, being close to Him seems just too good to be true. For some reason, they cannot seem to capture the magic. But then, when you look at their life, you see:

No Bible. No prayer. No seeking God's heart.

No passion. No longing. No room for the whispers.

Noise.

Their days are an endless flow of meaningless noise, and they wonder why they don't hear from God. It was J. Oswald Sanders who said, "We are at this moment as close to God as we really choose to be. True, there are times when we would like to know a deeper intimacy, but when it comes to the point, we are not prepared to pay the price involved."[32]

Tell me this: Are you willing to do what is necessary to be close to God? Are you willing to pay the price involved? What if that price is getting quiet? If we're being honest, even when we listen to faith-based podcasts, sermons, or worship songs, we are not leaving space for personal interaction. We worship God, we study God, but do we ever wait on God? Do we sit in silence to hear His agenda? It is in these moments that our lives can slow down, and that is why our Savior sought silence so frequently.

THE VOLUME OF JESUS

Throughout the gospel accounts, we often see Jesus retreating to the wilderness. Even the Son of God grew tired of crowds. And what did Jesus do to reset? He refreshed Himself with silence and solitude. Most Christians today neglect these practices.

As His influence increased and His calendar filled, Jesus never lost sight of the importance of silence. If anything, the Gospels reveal that Jesus valued silence increasingly as time went on. As John Mark Comer writes:

> In Luke's gospel in particular, you can chart Jesus' life along two axis points: the busier and more in demand and famous Jesus became, and the more he withdrew to his quiet place to pray . . . In seasons of busyness we need more time in the quiet place, not less.[33]

Busyness is not our excuse for dodging silence; it is our reason for needing silence. The faster life gets, the more stillness we need. Martin

—

The faster life gets, the

more stillness we need.

—

Luther is famous not just for his Ninety-Five Theses, but also for praying for three hours each day. (Don't worry, that is not going to be your challenge today!) When asked about his prayer life, Luther said, "I have so much business I cannot get on without spending three hours daily in prayer."[34] What might seem counterproductive to us—Luther's three hours of prayer—was actually necessary for Luther to fulfill all his duties. It was being silent before God, plugged into His whispers, that kept Luther effective and sane. He sat in silence before his King, and he changed the world in the process.

Our silence is a gift. Our silence is necessary. Our silence allows God to speak to our hearts. Our entertainment and noise and follies do the opposite. If we truly want to connect with the Lord, our first step is killing the noise.

TODAY'S CHALLENGE

Spend ten minutes in silence.

Find a place where you can be alone and undistracted (e.g., a park bench, a porch swing, a car in the driveway) and set a timer for ten minutes.

The goal of this silence is not to empty your mind, control your breathing or heart rate, or anything else that feels super spiritual. The goal of this silence is peace and simplicity.

Don't overthink it. Just enjoy!

YOUR OBEDIENCE

If you love Me, you will keep My commandments.
—JOHN 14:15 NASB

Y ou might be tempted to think that this chapter will be cold. When reading the word "obedience," some minds might think of the domineering father, the mean sports coach, or those teachers in movies who slap kids with yardsticks. While this response would be understandable, you need not be worried. The true believer understands the blessing of obedience. In obedience, we not only give our allegiance to God, but we also get blessings in return. Obedience is simply love in action, but it is a love that has to be learned.

WHAT CAUSES OBEDIENCE?

Obedience is not very complicated. When any command is made, the recipients of that command will ask themselves two questions. First, *What do I think about this person?* and second, *Do they have the authority to punish me?* Those are the two factors that determine obedience: your affection and their authority.

For the sake of illustration, let us pretend that a criminal is caught in the act of robbery. The policeman says, "Freeze!" But the criminal does not always freeze, does he? Of course not. Some people obey, and some do not. It is in this moment—that few-second gap between command and response—that the robber weighs affection and authority. Because the policeman has the authority to make this command, the criminal's affection will determine his move. Does he stop in his tracks and obey the police, or does he choose to rebel and take off on foot? Instinctively, the criminal asks himself, *What do I think about this cop? What is the risk if I do not obey?*

While I doubt that you will ever find yourself in this situation, your actions are still governed by the very same principle. Anytime someone makes a demand of you, you will weigh both affection and authority. How you eventually respond is the result of that exercise.

To give you a visual illustration of this thought experiment, take a look at the image below. This image has helped me to greatly simplify my thoughts on obedience. I call it the "Obedience Matrix."

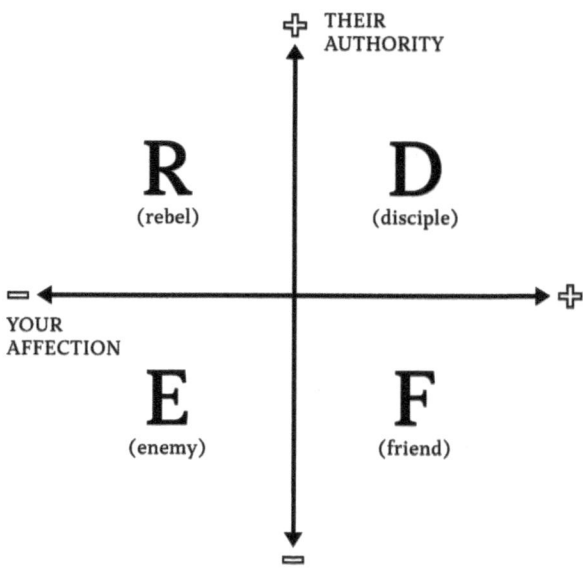

(You obey on the right side and disobey on the left side.)

(They have authority on the top portion and no authority on the bottom portion.)

It is this simple relationship between affection and authority that gives us four possible outcomes. I call them the rebel, the enemy, the disciple, and the friend. Let us talk about each of them in turn.

- **The Rebel** (*low affection, high authority*): This person disobeys a command that they know they should follow. They disobey as an act of defiance. The rebel operates out of selfishness, evil, hate, and jealousy (e.g., the rebellious child, the criminal who runs, or Satan when relating to God).
- **The Enemy** (*low affection, low authority*): This person simply disobeys as a matter of choice. Because the commander lacks the authority to punish, he disobeys the command just to spite him. The enemy operates out of disregard, disdain, and lack of respect (e.g., the sports opponent, the rival gang member, or Satan when relating to humans).
- **The Disciple** (*high affection, high authority*): This person is a willing student who loves his teacher. He recognizes the rightful authority of the commander, and he delights in following his commands. The disciple operates out of love and trust (e.g., the loving child, the well-trained dog, and yes, the single-minded Christian).
- **The Friend** (*high affection, low authority*): This person obeys a command not because he has to but simply because he wants to. While the commander has no true authority over him, he complies to please the commander. The friend operates out of love, kindness, and compassion (e.g., the parent who helps a child, the teacher who helps a student, or the child who is kind to a sibling).

Rebel, enemy, disciple, friend. These are our options. With these four characters in mind, let's see what the Bible has to say about our obedience.

THE CHRISTIAN'S CALL TO OBEDIENCE

The person who truly loves God—and therefore has a genuine faith—will show a consistent pattern of obedience. This does not mean that a Christian never sins, but there should be a general pattern of godliness. The greatest proof of genuine faith is a changed life—your thoughts are different; your actions are different. Not only that, but the Christian is also grieved when he falls into sin. He hates his sin because he loves Jesus. This is one mark of the legitimate Christian. After all, it was Jesus Himself who said:

> If you hold to my teaching, you are really my disciples.
> (John 8:31 NIV)

> If you love me, you will keep my commandments.
> (John 14:15)

> Anyone who loves me will obey my teaching.
> (John 14:23 NIV)

Who are really the disciples of Jesus? It is not those who merely have words and feelings, it is those who actually obey. A person's obedience is the proof of their love. Obedience is a great measure of your love for God because obedience costs you something. When the Bible tells you to do something that you don't want to do—like loving your enemy, forgiving the person who hurt you, and so on—obedience is not naturally easy. And that is where obedience costs you something. By obeying Jesus, you lose out on revenge. By obeying Jesus, you can't hold a grudge.

Church attendance does not prove we are Christians. Knowledge of the Bible does not prove we are Christians. Obedience, however, does. A Christian is someone who obeys the Lord. Our daily actions reveal our allegiance. It is only through consistent action that our faith is proven. This is why Jesus could ask:

> Now why do you call Me, "Lord, Lord," and do not do what I say? Everyone who comes to Me and hears My words and acts on them, I will show you whom he is like: he is like a man building a house, who dug deep and laid a foundation on the rock; and when there was a flood, the river burst against that house and yet it could not shake it, because it had been well built. But the one who has heard and has not acted accordingly is like a man who built a house on the ground without a foundation; and the river burst against it and it immediately collapsed, and the ruin of that house was great. (Luke 6:46–49 NASB)

So then, what do you see when you look in the mirror? Do you see a consistent pattern of obedience to Jesus? Do you see the obvious fruits of a true, saving faith? Actions speak louder than words when it comes to God's kingdom. As Maya Angelou once said, "When people show you who they are, believe them." The obedient person is the one who loves Jesus.

—

Church attendance does not prove we are Christians. Knowledge of the Bible does not prove we are Christians. Obedience does.

—

WHY DOES GOD DEMAND OUR OBEDIENCE?

At this point, you might be asking yourself: *Why does God have to be so strict? Why would God demand our obedience?* In reality, the fact that God is so strict and adamant about His law is actually to our benefit. He demands our obedience to increase our perfection, and He demands our obedience to further His plan.

Because God has a specific story that He plans to write, He uses obedient characters to carry out His plot. A great example of this is the story of David, who was crowned as king because of his character. Because God could trust him, God gave him the throne. Here is how the apostle Paul relayed that story:

> Fellow Israelites and you Gentiles who worship God, listen to me! The God of the people of Israel chose our ancestors; he made the people prosper during their stay in Egypt; with mighty power he led them out of that country . . . Then the people asked for a king, and he gave them Saul son of Kish, of the tribe of Benjamin, who ruled forty years. After removing Saul, he made David their king. God testified concerning him: "I have found David son of Jesse, a man after my own heart; he will do everything I want him to do." (Acts 13:16–17, 21–22 NIV)

Why was David chosen as a replacement for Saul? It was not because David attended church or because of his robust Old Testament knowledge. David was known as a man after God's own heart. He was chosen because he loved God, and God knew that because he obeyed.

God also demands our obedience because He wants us to reflect His character, and the commandments of God reveal that character. God possesses the ultimate love, kindness, wisdom, and strength, and

Jesus of Nazareth embodied those attributes. God wants us to obey Him so that we can be like Him, and He wants us to be like Him because He is perfect. In the words of C. S. Lewis:

> The command *Be ye perfect* is not idealistic gas. Nor is it a command to do the impossible. He is going to make us into creatures that can obey that command . . . If we let Him—for we can prevent Him, if we choose—He will make the feeblest and filthiest of us into a god or goddess, a dazzling, radiant, immortal creature, pulsating all through with such energy and joy and wisdom and love as we cannot now imagine, a bright stainless mirror which reflects back to God perfectly (though, of course, on a smaller scale) His own boundless power and delight and goodness.[35]

God tells us exactly how He wants to be loved. It is not confusing, nor is it complex. We obey God's commands as a matter of choice; we obey God's commands because of our love.

As we bring this chapter to a close, let's finish with the timeless words of King Solomon, who provides a perfect summation of our call to obedience. He writes:

> Now all has been heard; here is the conclusion of the matter: Fear God and keep his commandments, for this is the duty of all mankind. (Ecclesiastes 12:13 NIV)

—

Fear God and keep his commandments, for this is the duty of all mankind.

—ECCLESIASTES 12:13 NIV

—

TODAY'S CHALLENGE

Answer the following questions:

What is one area of your life where you willingly obey God, even though others might find it difficult?

_____

_____

_____

_____

What is one area of your life where you struggle to obey God, even though you know you are living in sin?

_____

_____

_____

_____

YOUR JUDGMENT AND TOLERANCE

Evil men do not understand justice, but those who
seek the Lord understand it completely.
—PROVERBS 28:5

I grew up in a home of attorneys. My father is an attorney. His father was an attorney. My aunt and two uncles are attorneys. My brother and sister are attorneys. Needless to say, in the Wheatley house that I grew up in, there was a heavy importance on the rule of law. It is an attorney's job to fight for the truth. They toil in the fields of right and wrong. If you have spent any time in a courtroom or legal office, you likely would have noticed a common symbol. That symbol is known as "Lady Justice." Lady Justice has been used as a symbol in courtrooms for as long as we can remember. Different renditions of her include *Justitia* of ancient Rome, *Dike* of Greece, and *Isis* of Egypt. I have provided an example for you here:

LADY JUSTICE

— THE SCALES
OF JUSTICE

My point here is not to give you a history lesson on courtroom symbols, but rather, to highlight the features that make up this character. First, you will notice that Lady Justice holds a sword in her right hand, which symbolizes her power to punish the sinner. Second, Lady Justice has a blindfold over her eyes, which allows her to judge without bias or prejudice. And finally, Lady Justice also carries a set of scales—commonly known as the "scales of justice"—which represent the impartiality of the law. True justice shows no favoritism. A scale does not care what you *wish* to be true; its job is to tell you what *is*. Those scales will be our focus today.

THE SCALES OF JUDGMENT

Nobody wants to feel judged. Nobody wants to appear judgmental. The problem is, life is not a philosophy class. Life does not happen in the safety of a lab. When we are faced with the ugly and evil of this world, we are forced to make our own best judgments. In that respect, we are *always* judging, all the time. In order to handle this balancing act, I often think back on Lady Justice—the symbol that I learned in my childhood. But instead of the typical imagery of Justitia, Dike, or Isis, I actually envision that *Jesus* is holding the scales. I have taken to calling those scales—the ones held by Jesus—the "scales of judgment." An image is provided for you here:

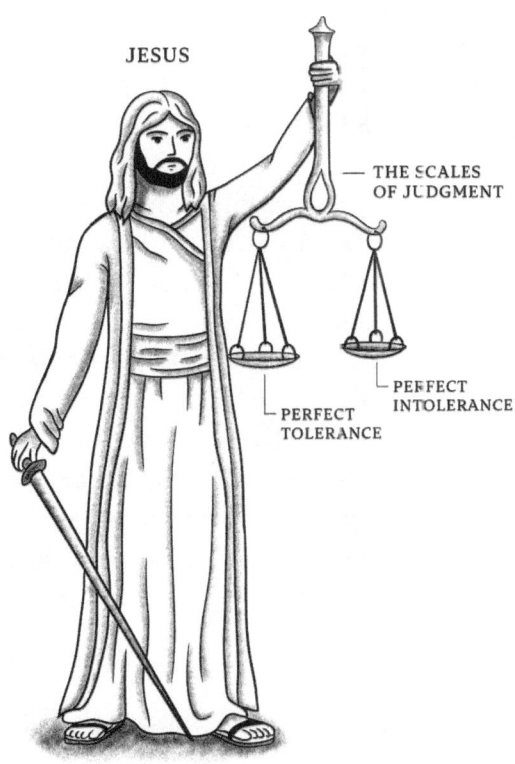

JESUS

THE SCALES OF JUDGMENT

PERFECT INTOLERANCE

PERFECT TOLERANCE

You will notice a few similarities between these two photos. In both images, we find a character in robes, a sword, and scales. Both people have the power to judge and convict. But this is where the similarities end. While Lady Justice is merely a symbol, Jesus of Nazareth was a man in history. His mother gave birth to Him. He had a job. He had friends. He paid taxes. He sweat and bled and laughed and cried. Jesus was a physical man who walked the earth.

The second difference, as I am sure you might have noticed, is that Jesus is not wearing a blindfold. Because Jesus is already the perfect judge, He needs no assistance from a piece of cloth. It is already His nature to exact perfect justice. As Moses wrote in the wilderness:

> He is the Rock, His work is perfect;
> For all His ways are justice,
> A God of truth and without injustice;
> Righteous and upright is He. (Deuteronomy 32:4 NKJV)

The final difference between these images of Lady Justice and Jesus is their scales. The Lady's scales of justice are both unlabeled—simply there to measure two sides of an argument. With Jesus' scales of judgment, however, each scale has a very clear label. I have labeled the two sides of His scales as "perfect tolerance" and "perfect intolerance." This symbolism has helped me understand just how Jesus judges, and how Christians should judge in response. The question to ask ourselves is this: *Do we love what God loves and hate what God hates?*

—
Do we love what God loves and hate what God hates?
—

PERFECT TOLERANCE

God is the most tolerant Being who has ever existed. No human who was, is, or ever will be is capable of acceptance like God. Throughout the story of the Bible, we see God initiating great acts of inclusion. Likewise, no group of people in the history of the world has been more inclusive than Christians. No clan has done more to unify the planet. After all, it was the Christians who elevated the status of women. It was the Christians who abolished the slave trade in the West. Just as God accepts men in all shapes and sizes, the children of God have followed His lead. That is why the Christian faith is, by definition, perfectly tolerant of all kinds of people. Whether Jew or Gentile, rich or poor, all humans are welcome to enter God's family. The apostle Paul explained it this way to the church in Galatia:

> For you are all sons and daughters of God through faith in Christ Jesus. For all of you who were baptized into Christ have clothed yourselves with Christ. There is neither Jew nor Greek, there is neither slave nor free, there is neither male nor female; for you are all one in Christ Jesus. (Galatians 3:26–28 NASB)

We all become one through our faith in Christ. According to Paul, there are no social statuses in the Christian church. Christians pay no attention to skin tones and bloodlines, nor are women to be treated as lesser than men. While we might have different gifts, talents, and roles in the church, our standing before God is always the same. We are sons and daughters through faith in Jesus. We are one. The apostle James added this on the subject of tolerance:

> My brothers, show no partiality as you hold the faith in our Lord Jesus Christ, the Lord of glory. For if a man wearing a gold ring and fine clothing comes into your assembly, and a

poor man in shabby clothing also comes in, and if you pay attention to the one who wears the fine clothing and say, "You sit here in a good place," while you say to the poor man, "You stand over there," or, "Sit down at my feet," have you not then made distinctions among yourselves and become judges with evil thoughts? (James 2:1–4)

The Bible leaves no room for judging a man's status. The worth of a human is determined by God, not by their job, income, or social standing. The Christian is called to be tolerant of all kinds of people, but we are also called to judge their behavior.

PERFECT INTOLERANCE

Although the Bible is perfectly clear about loving all humans, it is equally clear about hating all sin. Jesus was tolerant of people but intolerant of lawlessness. He had no trepidation in calling out wrongs. Sometimes, we Christians forget just how Jesus loved. Yes, He did always extend grace, kindness, and a listening ear, but Jesus would also eventually rebuke the sinner. That was the pattern set forth by our Lord: Give love to the sinner, then call for repentance.

Many of today's Christians, however, are too afraid to love like Jesus. In one breath, we claim to be God's "hands and feet," but in the next, we turn a blind eye to the sins of society. "Play the long game," we say. "They'll come around." This is the opposite approach of what God commands. As it says in the book of Proverbs:

Whoever says to the wicked, "You are in the right," will be cursed by peoples, abhorred by nations, but those who rebuke the wicked will have delight, and a good blessing will come upon them. (Proverbs 24:24–25)

And then, in the book of Isaiah:

> Woe to those who call evil good and good evil, who put darkness for light and light for darkness, who put bitter for sweet and sweet for bitter! (Isaiah 5:20)

And then, in the words of Paul:

> As for you, brothers, do not grow weary in doing good. If anyone does not obey what we say in this letter, take note of that person, and have nothing to do with him, that he may be ashamed. (2 Thessalonians 3:13–14)

The Christian is called to intolerance of what God forbids. He loves what God loves and hates what God hates. It was King Solomon who wrote, "The fear of the Lord is hatred of evil" (Proverbs 8:13). Therefore, it is kindness toward people and intolerance toward sin that actually leads to repentance. This is the balance that the Christian strikes when led by the Spirit and Scriptures. Here is how the Bible defines the scales of judgment:

It is kindness toward people and intolerance toward sin that actually leads to repentance.

Perfect Tolerance (of People):	*Perfect Intolerance (of Sin):*
Jew/Greek, slave/free, male/female, friend/enemy, marital status, financial status, intelligence, profession, etc. All humans are made in the image of God. (Galatians 3:28; Acts 10:34)	Murder, theft, lying, cheating, idolatry, adultery, homosexuality, fornication, pride, drunkenness, covetousness, taking the Lord's name in vain, etc. (1 Corinthians 6:9–10; 1 Timothy 1:8–10)

To Judge or Not to Judge?

The question, therefore, isn't whether or not we are called to judge. The question is *when* we are called to judge. Admittedly, the Bible gives some seemingly conflicting answers. For example, the apostle James says:

> God alone, who gave the law, is the Judge. He alone has the power to save or to destroy. So what right do you have to judge your neighbor? (James 4:12 NLT)

And the apostle Paul says:

> Therefore you have no excuse, O man, every one of you who judges. For in passing judgment on another you condemn yourself, because you, the judge, practice the very same things. (Romans 2:1)

But then, in stark contrast, the apostle John says:

> Everyone who goes on ahead and does not abide in the teaching of Christ, does not have God . . . If anyone comes to you and does not bring this teaching, do not receive him into your house or give him any greeting. (2 John 1:9, 10)

Is refusing to greet someone not judging their character? While greeting some people, we turn away others? That is certainly a judgment of character, but it is also commanded in Scripture. And if all Scripture is God-breathed (2 Timothy 3:16), how can we hold these commandments in tension? How do we govern our judgment and tolerance? While no person will do this perfectly, we'd be wise to remember Paul's letter to the Corinthians, where he puts our judgment in the proper place. He writes:

> It isn't my responsibility to judge outsiders, but it certainly is your responsibility to judge those inside the church who are sinning. God will judge those on the outside; but as the Scriptures say, "You must remove the evil person from among you." (1 Corinthians 5:12–13, NLT)

Christians are supposed to judge other Christians, and we can leave unbelievers to the judgment of God. But as we wrap up today's chapter, I can see how this subject matter might create a sense of idealism—a false dichotomy—between *judging* and *not judging* in your life. I understand how the line between them might appear a bit hazy. So, just to keep things as simple as possible, let's always remember the words of Jesus, who had this to say on the subject of judgment:

> Judge not, and you shall not be judged. Condemn not, and you shall not be condemned. Forgive, and you will be forgiven. Give, and it will be given to you . . . For with the same measure that you use, it will be measured back to you. (Luke 6:37, 38 NKJV)

There will be a Judge with a final judgment.
But it will not be you or I.

TODAY'S CHALLENGE

Answer the following questions:

Who are some people in your life that you need to be more tolerant of?

_____

_____

_____

What are some areas of your life that you need to be less tolerant?

_____

_____

_____

How might this "perfect intolerance" affect your life positively?

_____

_____

_____

How might this "perfect intolerance" affect your life negatively?

_____

_____

_____

YOUR FORGIVENESS

For if you forgive others their trespasses, your heavenly Father
will also forgive you, but if you do not forgive others their
trespasses, neither will your Father forgive your trespasses.
—MATTHEW 6:14–15

God is, by nature, a forgiving God. In any conversation about forgiveness, we first must begin with the forgiveness of God. When we ask the question, "How can a good God allow so much evil in the world?" there are a number of ways one can answer. One reason why God allows so much evil in the world is actually *because* of His love. Said differently, God's forgiveness is why so much evil persists. Here is what I mean:

Imagine, for a moment, that God is a king. (I am speaking of kings in the literal sense.) Like all kings, God would likely rule a kingdom that spanned many miles, but He would also have a home—a palace. Like all palaces, God's home would be beautifully decorated, with gold and silver and jewels all around. He would have beautiful sculptures and tapestries. His servants would wait on His every need. (This is what one expects in the home of a king.)

But then, imagine if God invited criminals to the palace, allowing the worst citizens of the land to visit and dine. Imagine if He sent word far and wide—to the caves, to the deserts, to the gutters, to the sewers—so that each citizen had an opportunity to meet Him.

Imagine if, once the guests arrived at the palace, all hell broke loose. They continued in their criminal ways. They stole all the gold. They destroyed all the tapestries. They went to the bathroom, but not in the bathroom. They ate all the food, ripped up the couches, and never once found the king to say thank you.

Imagine then, finally, as the hoodlums prepared to leave the palace, the King stood at the door to bid them goodbye. He does not say a word about the mess that they've made. He simply smiles at each one and says, "Come back tomorrow."

That is the world that you and I live in. That is why so much evil exists. God is the king, the world is His palace, and we are the ones who are wrecking His furniture. Day after day, year after year, God *allows* our evil as an act of forgiveness. We are those wretched creatures that God found in the gutter, but He always invites us back to the palace. He is constantly giving us grace upon grace. As it says in the book of Psalms:

> He does not deal with us according to our sins, nor repay us according to our iniquities. For as high as the heavens are above the earth, so great is his steadfast love toward those who fear him; as far as the east is from the west, so far does he remove our transgressions from us. As a father shows compassion to his children, so the Lord shows compassion to those who fear him. For he knows our frame; he remembers that we are dust. (Psalm 103:10–14)

The reason why God continues to forgive us is because of His long-term perspective. A spoiled meal or a broken couch is not the end of God's world. He forgives us, over and over, in order to give us more chances. He leaves the door open for us to repent. There are, however, some conditions we must meet to receive God's forgiveness. Much like a complimentary ticket that a friend leaves at will call, God's mercy and grace are always unmerited. We can do nothing to earn God's forgiveness, and we can do nothing to deserve God's forgiveness. The "ticket" He leaves us is always free. However, if there was a literal free ticket waiting at will call, then we would still have to get to the event venue, be there on time, have the right name that matches the ticket, and so on. It is much the same with the forgiveness of God. While His forgiveness is free, there is a process to release it that is laid out by Scripture. First of all, Jesus tells us:

> *As far as the east is from the west, so far does he remove our transgressions from us.*
>
> —PSALM 103:12

> If you forgive others their trespasses, your Heavenly Father will also forgive you, but if you do not forgive others their trespasses, neither will your Father forgive your trespasses. (Matthew 6:14–15)

And then, the apostle John adds:

> If we confess our sins, he is faithful and just to forgive us our sins and to cleanse us from all unrighteousness. (1 John 1:9)

And finally, the writer of Hebrews says:

> If we go on sinning deliberately after receiving the knowledge of the truth, there no longer remains a sacrifice for sins. (Hebrews 10:26)

There are three conditions to be met to receive God's forgiveness. The "ticket" is free and undeserved, but we still have to get to will call. God promises to forgive us, each and every time, if we meet the following conditions:

- If we forgive those who have sinned against us (Matthew 6:14–15)
- If we confess our sins and our need for forgiveness (1 John 1:9)
- If we don't sin deliberately and take God's mercy for granted (Hebrews 10:26)

Our Call to Forgiveness

In a country as prideful as our own, forgiveness is not a popular thing. We often teach our young to hold onto offenses. Our gurus have the temerity to call such things virtuous. In fact, I can recall driving one afternoon in southern California, and I saw a billboard on the highway that caught my eye. In big, bold letters, it said, "The Greatest Revenge Is Massive Success." My heart sank a little when I read that billboard. It encapsulates the American ethos perfectly. In America, we push to succeed, no matter the cost. We hold onto grudges as long as they serve us. This is why we remember that coach who cut us in high school. This is why, two months after a nasty breakup, we reveal "revenge bodies" on social media. We want to hurt the person who hurt us. We simply refuse to forgive and move on.

The vengeful person makes a grave mistake in assuming he is judge and jury. We have not been crowned as "keepers of the sword." While personal revenge does play well in the movies, the Bible commands us to do the opposite. It is not right for the Christian to seek revenge. As the apostle Paul once said to the Romans, "Never take your own revenge, beloved, but leave room for the wrath

of God, for it is written: 'VENGEANCE IS MINE, I WILL REPAY'"
(Romans 12:19 NASB). The Christian is not allowed to act like
James Bond. We do not hold grudges, and we do not settle scores.
The Christian leaves room for the wrath of God. While James Bond
might kill, the Christian forgives.

I once heard it said that we are never more like God than when we
forgive. While we are certainly like God when we create something,
or when we rear and raise children, or when we exercise dominion
over the animal kingdom, there is perhaps no aspect of God more
entirely radical than when He forgives the sinner. It is the act of forgiving the undeserved—an act we refer to as *mercy*—that seems so
irrational to us. We want to cause pain to the one who has pained us.
We want to get even. "Give 'em a taste of their own medicine," as they
say. But not God. God is, in His very nature, a God of forgiveness.
Perhaps this is why He allows pain in our life—He is trying to teach
us forgiveness. How else can we sinners adopt that habit? It was Jesus
Himself who said:

> You have heard that it was said, "You shall love your neighbor
> and hate your enemy." But I say to you, love your enemies
> and pray for those who persecute you, so that you may be
> sons of your Father who is in heaven. For he makes his sun
> rise on the evil and on the good, and sends rain on the just
> and on the unjust. For if you love those who love you, what
> reward do you have? Do not even the tax collectors do the
> same? And if you greet only your brothers, what more are you
> doing than others? Do not even the Gentiles do the same? You
> therefore must be perfect, as your heavenly Father is perfect.
> (Matthew 5:43–48)

The Gospel Heart

We are called to forgive because God forgives. We are called to display the gospel heart. The gospel heart gives when it is undeserved, and it forgives when it is undeserved. That is why Jesus, hanging on the cross, could so audaciously say, "Father, forgive them, for they know not what they do" (Luke 23:34).

What if, instead of locking someone up in their ugly past, we encouraged them into a brighter future?

What if you and I chose to forgive that way? What if, instead of locking someone up in their ugly past, we encouraged them into a brighter future?

When a puppy pees in the house, we might be upset for a moment, sure, but we forgive him quickly because he "knows not what he does." Likewise, when a baby cries for hours on end, we forgive that baby without hesitation—she, too, "knows not what she does." The question is, can we act like Jesus—seeing the puppy, the baby, or the person who wrongs us—and have a willingness to see them like He does? All of us humans are sinful by nature, and our actions can often hurt people. Jesus knows this truth far better than we do, and He showed us what it means to forgive.

Let us be people who understand our sinfulness.

Let us be people who forgive our debtors.

TODAY'S CHALLENGE

Complete this forgiveness exercise. Fill in the blanks.

I am mad at _____
(NAME)

because _____ .
(ACTION)

I am feeling _____
(NEGATIVE EMOTIONS)

because of how they treated me. Even still, I know that I am called to forgive. I know that in one hundred years I will not feel the pain of this wound.

As of today, _____ ,
(DATE)

I am choosing to release _____
(NAME)

to the judgment of God. Whether God gives them forgiveness or wrath, I trust that God is a better judge than I am and that He is more capable of handling this than me. I am choosing to be a person of forgiveness because I know that I myself have been forgiven.

STRENGTH

DAY TWENTY-FOUR

YOUR WORK

My Father is always working, and so am I.
—JOHN 5:17 NLT

There is a growing misconception in the church today. That misconception is both well-intentioned and easily remedied, but it is still a misconception, nonetheless. You have likely met Christians who will hold to this teaching, or perhaps you've read books that will advocate this thought. The misconception that misleads so many is this:

Humans, by nature, are beings of rest.

While this thought might seem novel and righteous, it is incomplete in its doctrine and can lead to laziness. In that sense alone, one can contend that this stance is unbiblical, and these next few pages will explain just why. The fact is, human beings, like God, are not made to operate from a place of rest. Human beings, on the contrary, are made to work.

THE NATURE OF WORK

The first verb in the Bible is one of creation. In Genesis 1:1, the Bible begins by saying this: "In the beginning, God created the heavens and the earth." You likely have heard this verse before. But notice what Genesis 1:1 does not say. It does not say that God rested or slept *before* He created. That sequence of events is not insignificant. Said differently, our first introduction to God is not as a God of rest, but rather, as a God of work. The first thing God did was work, not rest. Now, to be clear, God still rested on the seventh day, but the only reason He rested was *because* of His work. Even though God could never fatigue, nor does He ever slumber or sleep (Psalm 121:4), He still saw it fitting to rest for one day. It was time for God to enjoy—to revel in—the work of His hands. Rest is the natural *response* to work.

While God is certainly in favor of rest, His prevailing nature is one of work. He is a worker who rests, not a "rester" who works. As Tim Keller reminds us:

> In the beginning . . . God worked. Work was not a necessary evil that came into the picture later, or something human beings were created to do but that was beneath the great God himself. No, God worked for the sheer joy of it. Work could not have a more exalted inauguration.[36]

Work, at its core, is a very good thing. It is fulfilling to us and a service to others. It is necessary. We see this clearly reflected in the ministry of Jesus. Being one with the God who "never sleeps," Jesus was also a man of action. He lived a quiet life until He was thirty, but Jesus' eventual ministry was filled with labor. He traveled to and fro. He taught people. He healed people. Jesus was certainly a man of work, keeping an arduous schedule for His three years of ministry.

On one occasion, Jesus continued His work on the Sabbath day, and the Pharisees were appalled by His actions. The same Jesus who had once given the law to Moses—Jesus is one with the Father, after all—was making an amendment to His previous statutes. Now, He declared, God's followers were allowed to work on the Sabbath. We can read what happened next in the gospel of John:

> So the Jewish leaders began harassing Jesus for breaking the Sabbath rules. But Jesus replied, "My Father is always working, and so am I . . . I tell you the truth, the Son can do nothing by himself. He does only what he sees the Father doing. Whatever the Father does, the Son also does." (John 5:16–17,19 NLT)

Human beings are made in the image of God. Our Father is a worker. He is *always* working. In that respect, human beings are not created to wait or rest; we are created to work and to do. Like the God we reflect, we are workers who rest, not "resters" who work. In fact, we will even do work in heaven, as the Bible claims that we will rule over angels and help Christ run His kingdom (1 Corinthians 6:2–3). Just like Eden, the new earth will be perfect. Just like Eden, God's children will work.

—

We are workers who rest, not "resters" who work.

—

THE CURSE OF WORK

Some Christians feel that working hard and getting uncomfortable is somehow unrighteous or ungodly. It is not. The discomfort we experience in work is not the "badness" of it, it is simply the curse that has fallen upon work. When Adam and Eve rebelled against

God, sin entered the world, and our work was ruined. It was then that God said to Adam:

> Cursed is the ground because of you; through painful toil you will eat food from it all the days of your life. It will produce thorns and thistles for you, and you will eat the plants of the field. By the sweat of your brow you will eat your food until you return to the ground, since from it you were taken; for dust you are and to dust you will return. (Genesis 3:17–19 NIV)

There were no "thorns and thistles" in the Garden of Eden. The work was good and the harvest was plentiful. But then, sin arrived. Our work was cursed, and so was our harvest. While it is still in our nature to be people of work, we are combatted with toil as we do that work. Our land and bodies are working against us. Every walk is uphill; every resource is limited. The game has been rigged against its players.

It is this uphill battle that causes work to be difficult. This leads sinful humans to become lazy and whiny. This is not a new problem, of course, as we humans have been lazy since God rained down His curses. This is why the Bible warns us against succumbing to laziness, teaching that a harvest only comes through our diligent work. It says things like:

> The soul of the sluggard craves and gets nothing, while the soul of the diligent is richly supplied. (Proverbs 13:4)

> Work brings profit, but mere talk leads to poverty! (Proverbs 14:23 NLT)

> Love not sleep, lest you come to poverty; open your eyes, and you will have plenty of bread. (Proverbs 20:13)

There is another type of work that is equally foolish. While some people are lazy—avoiding their work—other people are actually *too* good at working. We call these people workaholics. They are not lazy; they are the opposite—they love their work! They love their work too much, in fact. This is especially true of American workers.

Some Americans are so good at work that we worship them for it. We see this the most with celebrity athletes, motivational speakers, and military men. We always use the same word—*obsessed*—to describe these people, and we adore and praise them on account of their work ethic. The truth is, most of these athletes and moguls are chasing a fantasy. In the deepest parts of their soul, they believe that work brings money, money brings power, power brings options, and options bring rest. Money, power, options, rest. They hope that their discipline can bring them to paradise. But all of their efforts are acts of futility. They are racing up mountains in search of the moon. It was the great King Solomon—a man best known for his power and riches—who said this about chasing achievements:

> And I saw that all toil and all achievement spring from one person's envy of another. This too is meaningless, a chasing after the wind . . . Better one handful with tranquility than two handfuls with toil. (Ecclesiastes 4:4, 6 NIV)

This is the conflict that we face in work. If we work too little, we get poor results; if we work too much, we labor like fools. We cannot enjoy the fruits of our labor. But if this is true, how can we renew the passion that God has given us? How should we Christians plan our work?

—

If we work too little,

we get poor results;

if we work too much,

we labor like fools.

—

201

THE RHYTHM OF WORK

Work is a part of life. For most of us, work takes up more of our time than any other thing—more than sleep, recreation, or anything else. But if work is a very good thing under a very bad curse, how then should we treat our work? What should work look like in our everyday lives? The Bible has much to say on this subject, but I would summarize it all in this statement:

Work comes first on the calendar, but not in priority.

Our work comes first in terms of our duties. This does not mean that work comes before God or family in terms of priorities, but it does come before moments of leisure. Our work comes first, and fun comes later. We get the job done, and then we relax. By choosing to do the difficult things first, we are setting ourselves up for a bountiful harvest. If we choose the difficult now, our future is comfortable; if we choose the comfortable now, our future is difficult. It is the timeless law of sowing and reaping, and it applies to all of God's creatures. As King Solomon writes:

> Go to the ant, you lazy one,
> Observe its ways and be wise,
> Which, having no chief,
> Officer, or ruler,
> Prepares its food in the summer
> And gathers its provision in the harvest.
> How long will you lie down, you lazy one?
> When will you arise from your sleep? (Proverbs 6:6–9 NASB)

Even though the ant has no manager, master, or ruler to govern it, it still does its job with precision. It prepares its food, gathers its supplies, and then enjoys its harvest. King Solomon's lesson from the ant is simple: When a man is lazy, his harvest is poor. When you are lax in your work, you receive little fruit.

In the same way, many people pray and ask God to bless them financially. They want better pay, better jobs, and better lives. For many of these people, however, God refuses to answer their prayers. Why? Because they ignore the law of sowing and reaping They simply refuse to do the work. Let's not forget, it was God Himself who set up this law, and ignoring it is a product of laziness. If you are asking God to bless you but not doing the work, then you can't be surprised when the fruit is not plentiful. We can pray all we want, but God doesn't move if we don't move, either. He expects us to hold up our end of the bargain.

Do you want to be well-compensated? Do you want to have great impact on the world? Hone your craft, improve your skills, and develop your work into mastery. *Be incredibly proficient in your work.* As the Bible asks rhetorically, "Do you see a man who excels in his work? He will stand before kings" (Proverbs 22:29 NKJV).

Because God is a worker, He wants us to be workers. A Christian should earn the food he eats. We Christians are not mooches, and we are not busybodies. We do the work and enjoy the process. Like Jesus before us, we are working because our Father is working. Work is our call to the service of others. But while we are workers by nature, we still work at God's pace. We never work to the point of chaos or burnout. The apostle Paul understood this balance, telling the disciples to:

> Make it your goal to live a quiet life, minding your own business and working with your hands, just as we instructed you before. (1 Thessalonians 4:11 NLT)

The Christian life is a simple life. It is the quiet life. When we mind our own business and do our work first, then everyone partakes in our harvest.

We all have a heavenly work to accomplish. As the apostle Paul once wrote, "We are God's handiwork, created in Christ Jesus to do good works, which God prepared in advance for us to do" (Ephesians 2:10 NIV). Just as God has been working from the very beginning, we also should work in the very same way. We relentlessly serve from the best of our talents. Our work is the way that we give of ourselves.

You, my friend, were made to work. You were made to bless those around you with your time and talent. If you obey God's commands and reflect His image, then your joy in work will be great.

Let it be said of us, like the Father and Son:

We Christians are always working.

TODAY'S CHALLENGE

Do some work today that you truly enjoy.

Perhaps you can do some gardening, some yard work, you can shovel some snow, you can cook up a meal for your favorite people, or anything else that brings you joy.

Just remember, while it has to be work, it has to be fun. And then watch that work bless you and others!

DAY TWENTY-FIVE

YOUR REST

Come to me, all you who are weary and burdened, and I will give you rest.
—MATTHEW 11:28 NIV

Our God is a God of work. We discussed that yesterday at length. He creates, builds, and holds things together. He does this constantly. As the psalmist once wrote, "Indeed, he who watches over Israel never slumbers or sleeps" (Psalm 121:4 NLT). But while God might never slumber or sleep, He is certainly capable of rest. He wants His children to rest as well, and that is the subject of this chapter.

A CHANGE OF PACE

After God created the universe in six days, He decided to rest on the seventh. He did this not because He needed to, but simply because He wanted to. After a good week of work, a full day of rest can be equally satisfying. If work is the process, rest is the product.

But if we are being honest, rest can feel inefficient at times. Can it not? If we are resting, we are not achieving! If we are resting, we are not improving! And the American life does not do us any favors, as our fast-paced, always-get-ahead, no-days-off kind of culture is in no way conducive to rest. You'd think it would be the opposite! Between our air conditioning, automatic dishwashers, electric lighting, and food delivery services, never in history have we had more free time. Even still, so few of us enjoy the rest that God wants for us. Sometimes the busyness of life can get us distracted. We see an example of this in Mary and Martha—two sisters in the Bible who were companions with Jesus.

In the gospel of Luke, we hear of a time when Jesus entered a certain village, and He was then invited to come to the house of Martha. Once Jesus had entered her home, Martha began preparing supper. But her sister, Mary, was focused on different things. Here is how Luke describes that scene:

> And she had a sister called Mary, who sat at the Lord's feet and listened to his teaching. But Martha was distracted with much serving. (Luke 10:39–40)

As Martha was busy preparing the meal, Mary was resting with Jesus. She was taking some time to enjoy His presence. This meant that Martha, much to her disgust, had lost her sous-chef and much-needed helper. The conversation that followed was quite enlightening, as it tells us about the Lord's feelings on rest. Leaving the kitchen to speak with Jesus, Martha said:

> "Lord, do you not care that my sister has left me to serve alone? Tell her then to help me." But the Lord answered her, "Martha, Martha, you are anxious and troubled about many things, but one thing is necessary. Mary has chosen the good portion, which will not be taken away from her." (Luke 10:40-42)

One sister was anxious and troubled; the other was simply with Jesus. One sister was busy at work; one sister was happy at rest. Which person are you? If you are anything like me, then your natural wiring is a bit like Martha's, trying to work and work your way out of trouble. Perhaps there is more for us to gain in the area of rest, and perhaps for us, less would be more.

A healthy life leaves room for rest. We need fun, joy, play, and tranquility. Even still, so many of us complain about being tired. We are overstimulated and overwhelmed. But tell me this: Why not schedule some time to be understimulated? When was the last time you were underwhelmed? Maybe instead of hitting the gym at 4:45 a.m., we can wake up at 6:30 a.m. and rise with the sun. Perhaps we can move slower, talk slower, eat slower, live slower. Maybe our existence can become one of rest. As we discussed yesterday, Paul was very direct in telling us to "make it your goal to live a quiet life" (1 Thessalonians 4:11 NLT).

How do we, as working people, find the right balance of rest in our lives? How can we enter that lasting peace? If we pause to remember our sister, Mary, the answer should make itself plain. Jesus is the Prince of Peace, and He always will offer us rest.

BREAKING THE SABBATH

For the second half of our discussion on rest, let us take a few minutes to cover the Sabbath. There have been a handful of books in recent memory that have popularized an observance of the Sabbath. Instead of spending their weekends watching football, running errands, or getting social, some Christians are now turning off their phones, getting very quiet, and spending more time with God. These are all good things! But as good as it is to spend time with God, the Bible prescribes nothing about what *day* we should do it.

There are two truths we must remember when discussing the Sabbath: First, Jesus never sinned, and second, Jesus broke the Sabbath. How can we hold those two things in tension? If Jesus did miracles on the Sabbath (John 9:14), if Jesus' disciples plucked grain on the Sabbath (Matthew 12:1–8), if Jesus compelled other people to work on the Sabbath (John 5:8–10)—all of which seemed to violate the Sabbath day—then one might start to understand why the Israelites were mad at Him. They saw Jesus as a heretic who was breaking their laws. In that sense, I suppose they were right to accuse Jesus of anarchy. Jesus *did* break the Sabbath. He *shattered* the Sabbath, in fact.

Because Jesus is the visible expression of the invisible God (Colossians 1:15), He maintains the authority to change God's commandments. Yes, that even includes the observance of the Sabbath. In fact, it was Jesus Himself who said, "The Son of Man is Lord of the Sabbath" (Matthew 12:8 NASB). As the Lord of the Sabbath, Jesus can do with the Sabbath whatever He pleases, which was why He broke its norms so consistently.

—

*Jesus did break the
Sabbath. He shattered
the Sabbath, in fact.*

—

Here is the reality: God cares more about our hearts than robotic rule-following. He cares more about loyalty than the state of our calendars. If the disciples picked grain on the Sabbath, fine. If Jesus healed someone's legs on the Sabbath, that was okay as well. Why? Because rules and statutes are subservient to love. As long as these "Sabbath-offenders" loved God in their hearts, Jesus was willing to look past the legalism. He cared more about the spirit than the rule of the law. In fact, there are a number of world-class, God-fearing Bible characters who never observed a Sabbath. I am not talking about some no-name pagan who was smote by God, I am talking about our favorite saints. Here are a few giants of the faith who never practiced a Sabbath:

Abraham and Isaac.

Enoch and Noah.

Jacob and Joseph.

Adam and Eve.

None of these people partook in a Sabbath. The Sabbath had not been invented when they walked the earth. They all loved God and they all had rest, but they could only love and rest with the revelation of their day.

After Adam and Eve were banned from the Garden, they knew God in part, and they rested in part. The next phase of revelation— the Sabbath day—was God's provision of rest for old covenant Israel. Much like the old covenant laws about washing and eating, the Sabbath would separate the Jews from neighboring nations. The point of the Sabbath, among other things, was to make Israel look different from the Gentiles. It also provided the Jews with a specific day each week (Saturday) to rest and commune with God. Just as God worked six days and rested the seventh, so too would the nation that followed Him.

The old covenant Sabbath was an earthly ritual meant to symbolize, foreshadow, and point Israel to her coming Messiah. But God had a third revelation in mind, granting you and me a deeper, more lasting rest than the Israelites. Through the finished work of Jesus on the cross, our rest is not just one day per week. Our rest is today, tomorrow, and till the end of time.

DEAD TO THE SABBATH,
AT REST IN CHRIST

Jesus came to fulfill the Law and all of its ordinances. Observing the Sabbath was one such ordinance. By fulfilling this old covenant day of rest, Jesus was replacing it with a greater method: Himself. The old covenant was complete, and a new covenant had come. As the writer of Hebrews explains:

Now if Joshua had succeeded in giving them this rest, God would not have spoken about another day of rest still to come. So there is a special rest still waiting for the people of God. For all who have entered into God's rest have rested from their labors, just as God did after creating the world. (Hebrews 4:8–10 NLT)

This is a truth that the Gentiles would come to know. Thanks to Jesus, we have broken away from the lesser practices, and we cling to the rest that He brings. While the old covenant believer had one day of rest, the new covenant believer has rest every day. Our rest does not come from longer naps, lighter schedules, or entering the Promised Land with Joshua. Our rest comes from the reality of knowing the Lord.

Our rest does not come from longer naps, lighter schedules, or entering the Promised Land with Joshua. Our rest comes from knowing the Lord.

Just as Jesus suffered and died for the sins of all men, He was raised from the dead for the *rest* of all men. We have rest because of His victory, not because of our schedules on one day per week. That is why Paul cut out the knees of the Sabbath in his writings, saying this to the Christians who lived in Colossae:

So don't let anyone condemn you for what you eat or drink, or for not celebrating certain holy days or new moon ceremonies or Sabbaths. For these rules are only shadows of the reality yet to come. And Christ himself is that reality. (Colossians 2:16–17 NLT)

Paul says we are not condemned when we do not observe. And why? Because our rest is not found on a day of the week, our rest can be found in Jesus. The Sabbath was a shadow, but Christ is the substance. It is also worth noting the Ten Commandments (do not murder, do not steal, etc.), wherein it is only the fourth commandment (remember the Sabbath and keep it holy) that is nowhere repeated by a New Testament writer. While every other commandment is covered elsewhere in the New Testament—and sometimes, at length—not one New Testament writer declares the Sabbath must continue. Not Peter, not Paul, not John, not Jesus. Here is why:

The Jews offered lambs to cover their sins. But *Jesus* is our Lamb.

The Jews ate manna as they wandered the wilderness. But *Jesus* is our Bread.

The Jews crowned David as their king. But *Jesus* is our King.

The Jews observed the Sabbath to find their rest. But *Jesus* is our Rest.

That was the point in Paul's letter to Colossae: Jesus is our rest, today and forever. But at the same time, just to make sure we cover all sides of the argument, Paul did take a slightly different stance when he was writing the Romans. These two letters do not conflict with each other, but they do serve to shave off Paul's sharper edges. Still speaking of the Sabbath, here is what Paul said to the Christians in Rome:

> Now accept the one who is weak in faith, but not to have quarrels over opinions. One person has faith that he may eat all things, but the one who is weak eats only vegetables . . . One person values one day over another, another values every day the same. Each person must be fully convinced in his own mind. The one who observes the day, observes it for the Lord, and the one who eats, does so with regard to the Lord. (Romans 14:1–2, 5–6 NASB)

What can we learn from the words of Paul? First, though all Christians are Christians in the deepest way, there are still some

Christians of a "weaker" faith. What does this mean? By reverting back to old covenant teachings, some Christians miss out on the freedoms afforded them. Perhaps they are Gentile Christians who eat only vegetables (thus avoiding the meats sacrificed to pagan idols). Or perhaps they are Jewish Christians observing the Sabbath (even though the practice of the Sabbath had been made obsolete).

—

Rest is the goal.

Religion is not.

—

The second thing we can learn is that even though Paul says the Sabbath is unnecessary, we are still welcome to observe it if we choose. In other words, we are free to observe this obsolete practice. (It is biblically permissible, but biblically unnecessary.) I do, however, have one caution for you. If you are someone who chooses to observe the Sabbath day, my hope is that this observation does not *rob* you of rest. Said differently, I hope that by feeling exceedingly spiritual and rested on Sundays, you are not lacking that same feeling on Wednesdays. The danger of observing a strict Sabbath is that it *does* feel spiritual. It can make that "Sabbath day" feel different from the others, as if that one special day is somehow more holy. It is not. Just as Jesus Christ is the same yesterday, today, and forever (Hebrews 13:8), so too is our rest.

Rest is the goal. Religion is not. Just like Adam, Eve, and Enoch before you, you do not need a Sabbath to be resting in God. The question, therefore, is not when, where, or how we rest. The question to ask is *Who* is our rest? According to Mary, and Paul, and Jesus Himself:

Our rest can be found in Him.

TODAY'S CHALLENGE

Grade yourself in the questions below.

On a scale of 1–10, how rested do you typically feel?

NOT AT ALL   COULD NOT BE BETTER!

On a scale of 1–10, how well do you understand the character of Jesus?

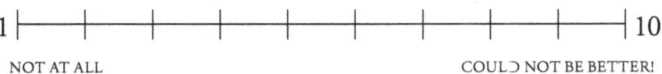

NOT AT ALL   COULD NOT BE BETTER!

On a scale of 1–10, how much rest do you feel *because* of Jesus?

NOT AT ALL   COULD NOT BE BETTER!

DAY TWENTY-SIX

YOUR APPEARANCE

But the LORD said to Samuel, "Do not look at his appearance or at the height
of his stature, because I have rejected him; for God does not see as man sees,
since man looks at the outward appearance, but the LORD looks at the heart."
—1 SAMUEL 16:7 NASB

I grew up in Orange County, California. While Orange County is probably best known for its beautiful weather, cultural diversity, and an endless array of great entertainment, it boasts an additional label that is not quite as flattering. If you asked people who grew up in other parts of the country—perhaps the South, the Midwest, or on the East Coast—they would paint a similar picture of the "California" stereotype. We Californians are known for our talent in snobbery. We care about superficial things and outward appearances—our cars, our careers, our bodies, and so on. With the influences of entertainment and money being so prevalent there, many Californians make a habit of pursuing physical beauty. The men chase it in women, and the women chase it for themselves.

With the increasing influence of social media, online dating, and the digitization of human relationships, this "California culture" is now spreading worldwide. Nowadays, it seems that our outward appearance and physical beauty have never been under more scrutiny. It is not uncommon for entire news stories to be written about a celebrity's outfit. We see prepubescent girls becoming stars on social media, exhibiting more cosmetic skills than a trained cosmetologist.

Americans are obsessed with physical appearance. For some of us, the strongest influence in our lives is not a friend, not a mentor, not a Bible, but a mirror. But this obsession with beauty is not a new thing.

THE GOOD, THE BAD, AND THE UGLY

God's creatures have been mistreating their beauty since the very beginning. It was this very obsession—an obsession with beauty—that caused Satan to rebel against God. That is where his downfall began. He was once a high-ranking angel, enriched by God with incredible blessings. As it says in the book of Ezekiel:

> You were the seal of perfection, full of wisdom and perfect in beauty. You were in Eden, the garden of God; every precious stone adorned you . . . Your heart became proud on account of your beauty, and you corrupted your wisdom because of your splendor. (Ezekiel 28:12–13, 17 NIV)

For some of us, the strongest influence in our lives is not a friend, not a mentor, not a Bible, but a mirror.

It was not Satan's beauty that made him evil; it was the pride in his heart that corrupted him. Satan had, for all intents and purposes, looked in a mirror, realized his beauty, and valued it more than he should have. He worshipped the gift instead of the Giver. He worshipped himself instead of his God.

Now, just to be fair, we should not turn a blind eye to the existence of beauty. Physical beauty does exist. It is a gift from God, and every human has it in varying degrees. In fact, there are a number of examples in Scripture where someone is specifically highlighted for their appearance. For instance, Job's daughters were the fairest in all the land (Job 42:15). Jacob's wife Rachel is recognized for her beauty in face and figure (Genesis 29:17). Nabal's wife, Abigail, was so intelligent and good-looking that David stole her away and took her as his own (1 Samuel 25:3). And then, lest we forget about the gentlemen, I'd be remiss to not mention Joseph, Moses, Absalom, and Daniel, all of whom are described in the Bible as handsome.

My point here is not to keep score in some biblical beauty contest. While physical beauty can exist in the world, our outward appearances are all gifts from God. Not one of us chose our height, our skin tone, or our parents' genetics. Not one of us chose how our bones were constructed. And yet, all of us can choose how our hearts are constructed, and that is how God measures beauty.

BEAUTY, IN THE EYE OF THE CREATOR

You have probably heard the phrase "beauty is in the eye of the beholder." A part of this adage is perfectly true. Beauty is, in fact, subjective. One person's likes are another's dislikes. One person's preference is another's pet peeve. And yet, the Bible puts forth a different maxim. For the Christian, true beauty is not found in the eye of the beholder. True beauty is found in the eye of the Creator. How God defines beauty is its true definition. Therefore, if we want to have a true conversation about appearance and beauty, we must understand those words as our Creator defines them.

> *True beauty is not found in the eye of the beholder. True beauty is found in the eye of the Creator.*

In a famous story from 1 Samuel 16, we catch a glimpse of how God defines the beauty of humans. The Creator sent a prophet—Samuel—to the city of Bethlehem, to the house of Jesse, to find a new king for Israel. As Jesse and his sons entered the room, Samuel's eyes quickly landed on Jesse's son, Eliab.

Surely, this is the one, Samuel thought (1 Samuel 16:6).

Let's be honest: This Eliab must have been quite the looker! Seriously, how else could Samuel have reached his conclusion? No words have been spoken at this point in the story. Perhaps Eliab was the tallest and strongest among his brothers? Or maybe he just had a great head of hair? Whatever the reason, Samuel clearly saw something appealing in Eliab, but God had a different idea. It was then that the Lord said to Samuel, "Do not look at his appearance or at the height of his stature, because I have rejected him; for God does not see as man sees, since man looks at the outward appearance, but the LORD looks at the heart" (1 Samuel 16:7 NASB).

Jesse made seven of his sons pass before Samuel. Just like God had done with Eliab, He passed on them all. "Are these all the sons you have?" Samuel asked.

"There is still the youngest," Jesse answered. "He is tending the sheep" (1 Samuel 16:11 NIV). Sure enough, the young shepherd boy turned out to be David. While David would eventually become a great warrior, he was only a lad when he first met Samuel. David was the youngest brother, the runt of the litter, but his heart loomed the largest before God. Upon seeing the boy, Samuel anointed David's head with oil, and he pronounced that David would be king in Israel. It was not physical attributes that God was after; it was a state of the heart that He cherished. One thousand years later, the apostle Paul shared this comment about what happened that day:

> After removing Saul, he made David their king. God testified concerning him: "I have found David son of Jesse, a man

after my own heart; he will do everything I want him to do."
(Acts 13:22 NIV)

While his predecessor, Saul, was tall and handsome, David was
known for his God-fearing heart. God made him the king because
of his character. The reason I share that story is this: We must learn
to value the beauty God values. We must cherish true beauty as seen
through God's eyes. Human beings are always judging and tweaking
our external casings, whereas God is concerned with our spirits therein.
The apostle Peter said this to the women of Asia:

> Your beauty should not come from outward adornment, such
> as elaborate hairstyles and the wearing of gold jewelry or
> fine clothes. Rather, it should be that of your inner self, the
> unfading beauty of a gentle and quiet spirit, which is of great
> worth in God's sight. (1 Peter 3:3–4 NIV)

God's measure of beauty is different than ours. He calls His daughters to have gentle, quiet, beautiful *spirits*. He cares more about their
character than the state of their hair. What Peter implies here is that
human beings—though in this case, specifically women—have an
"adornment" or "beauty" in the eyes of God. We do, in fact, possess a
beauty. The question, however, is where we decide that beauty will be.
Will it be an outward adornment—with elaborate hairstyles, expensive
jewelry, plastic surgeries, and more—or will it be an adornment of
the inner self, with a beauty that can travel to heaven?

THE SENSUAL STATES OF AMERICA

Our country is growing increasingly promiscuous. Our taste for
morality continues to wane. It might be hard to imagine this, but

it was just one hundred years ago that American women could be arrested at beaches for simply revealing their shoulders.[37] *Their shoulders!* Nowadays, women show up to work baring more skin than that. Unfortunately, when our men believe that beauty is only found in externals, our women feel tempted to peacock their bodies. Why not show off some skin if it lands you a man? This thinking—though devilish—has become so normal for us that we don't even notice it. But I would issue this caution to the female reader:

The bait with which you catch the man is what the man will crave.

Ladies, if a man sees you, and falls for you, and stays with you long-term—but only on account of your beauty or sexual prowess— then those are the things he will long for in marriage. Those are the things that will coax him to stay. But what happens when the wrinkles come? What happens when your body changes? What happens when you are tired and busy from raising your kids, and your sex life does not look the same? What then? What will he do?

The bait with which you catch the man is what the man will crave.

So then, to the female reader, I ask you this: Do you want men to see you as lovely and gentle, or is your reputation a bit more risqué? Would a life with you be based upon sex, or would it be a genuine pursuit of the soul? The choice is yours.

And to you, the male reader, I'd be remiss not to mention our failure of women. (I am writing these words to myself as well, as I should certainly be counted among the offenders.) Gentlemen, we have failed our sisters in the way that we treat them. We have grossly mishandled our God-given role. God tells us to cherish their internal spirits, yet we typically stop at their outward appearances. But why? Are we not more than animals? Is this really our best? Can we not raise our sights and start acting like men? You and I are faced with the challenge that confronts every male: Will our

—

The bait with which you catch the man is what the man will crave.

—

love or our lust be the victor? In his book *The Four Loves*, C. S. Lewis provides a chilling image of the lust-led man:

> We use a most unfortunate idiom when we say, of a lustful man prowling the streets, that he "wants a woman". Strictly speaking, a woman is just what he does not want. He wants a pleasure for which a woman happens to be the necessary piece of apparatus. How much he cares about the woman as such may be gauged by his attitude to her five minutes after fruition (one does not keep the carton after one has smoked the cigarettes.)[38]

Men, we are just as responsible for the state of our culture. There are plenty of women who are doing things well, and *men* are the ones who are failing. Many women are dressing modestly, living godly lives, yet we see them as something subhuman. They are that "necessary piece of apparatus." They are that cigarette carton we dispense after using. How quickly we forget to humanize women. In our lust, we forget that this woman—this daughter of God—was six years old at one point in time. She went to kindergarten. She had a lunch pail. She braided her hair and put Band-Aids on boo-boos. *She is a daughter.* Have we completely forgotten that image of innocence? Do we not care enough to remember that gift? The object of our lust might be thirty years old, she might make plenty of money, but she will always be a daughter of God.

Men, we so rarely praise women for their internal beauty that they greatly overvalue the externals. But no more. Let's handle our business, start acting like men, and see beauty in the eye of the Creator. In the words of King Lemuel, the God-fearing man knows that "charm is deceitful, and beauty is vain, but a woman who fears the Lord is to be praised" (Proverbs 31:30).

As we finish this chapter, let me leave you both—the male and female reader—with one final thought to consider. God says that our adornment is found in the internal person. If that is true, then we are much more likely to hear someone's beauty than we are to see it. We experience beauty by talking *to* someone, not merely by looking *at* someone. In that sense, we'd be more likely to experience beauty through a phone call than we would by looking at a photograph.

True beauty is not a physical reality.

It is a heavenly bent of the soul.

TODAY'S CHALLENGE

Write three things about yourself that reveal inner beauty.

If the Lord were to "look at your heart" like He did with David, what would He find? What would He say?

1) _____

_____

2) _____

_____

3) _____

_____

YOUR FOOD

And day by day, attending the temple together and breaking bread in their homes, they received their food with glad and generous hearts.
—ACTS 2:46

Of the many blessings that God has given us, very few rank higher than the blessing of food. Whether we are celebrating with friends or mourning a hardship, few things are as comforting as a warm meal can be. There are two questions to cover on the topic of food: First, according to the Bible, what foods should we Christians be eating today? And second, can the foods that we eat bring us closer to God? Those questions are our focus for today.

A HISTORY OF FOOD

Before we dive into all things diets and dining, we first must discuss the story of food. When you even read the word "food," you might be envisioning your favorite meal—maybe steak and potatoes, a cheeseburger and fries, or, for the health-conscious, a beautiful salad with every leaf known to man. However, it is still important for us to understand our diet and how it has changed over time. I have had a number of instances with friends and family where diet became a matter of contention. In one, a professing Christian chose to avoid all meat—and purely for the sake of the animals. Was she right to do that? Was she wrong? In another instance, a couple from church had chosen to become vegans, citing Adam and Eve's diet as their prime motivation. Naturally, I could not help but wonder: What has man eaten through the pages of history? What are we supposed to be eating today?

When God formed mankind, he created Adam and Eve to need food to sustain them. That much is obvious. But what did God give to them to be their food? Fruits, vegetables, nuts, and seeds. Here are God's words after the creation of Adam:

> Behold, I have given you every plant yielding seed that is on the surface of all the earth, and every tree which has fruit yielding seed; it shall be food for you. (Genesis 1:29 NASB)

That was man's diet for hundreds of years—fruits, vegetables, nuts, and seeds. But then, after a worldwide flood in the days of Noah (Genesis 6), God decided to update the menu of man, allowing humans to eat meat for the very first time. After the waters of the flood subsided, God said this to Noah:

> Every moving thing that is alive shall be food for you;
> I have given everything to you, as I gave the green plant.
> (Genesis 9:3 NASB)

In the eyes of God, eating animal flesh was no less humane than eating a squash or a cucumber. For some reason, still perfectly aligned with His flawless nature, God expanded man's diet to include other creatures. But then, hundreds of years later, God would eventually amend the menu again—for the humans who loved Him, that is.

By the fourteenth century BC, the Israelites were already known as God's chosen people. Some two million strong, they had just been freed from the whips of Egypt. Shortly after freeing the Israelites from Egyptian captivity, God created a code for His people to follow. He wanted them to act differently, dress differently, and, yes, even eat differently.

In both Leviticus 11 and Deuteronomy 14, God delivered specific food laws for the nation of Israel. They were permitted to eat some animals but forbidden from eating others. What animals were they called to avoid? While this list is not meant to be all-encompassing, some animals that were deemed "unclean" included the camel, the rabbit, the pig, the eagle, any fish without fins or scales, the falcon, the pelican, the bat (as if anyone had to be told!), the mouse, the crocodile, any four-legged animals that walked on their paws, and many more. God's reason for prescribing these vast restrictions went well beyond heartburn and calories. God's people were holy, and their diet would be holy. He created a diet to make them stand out from the pagans.

Then, about fifteen hundred years later, Jesus brought an end to these Mosaic food laws. During His earthly ministry, Jesus explained that the food laws were only ever a preamble—a shadow—of the truth that His coming would reveal. That future truth was upon them now: *God cares more about your heart than the food in your stomach.* Jesus says this in the gospel of Mark:

> "Do you not understand that whatever goes into the person from outside cannot defile him, because it does not go into his heart, but into his stomach, and is eliminated?" (Thereby He declared all foods clean.) And He was saying, "That which comes out of the person, that is what defiles the person." (Mark 7:18–20 NASB)

Here we have Jesus Christ—the visible expression of the invisible God (Colossians 1:15)—making another amendment to the menu of man. While God had once declared that rabbits and crocodiles could make an eater unclean, He was changing His tune with the words of Jesus. It was no longer what went into the mouth that could spoil a man, but rather, what came out of the mouth. What goes into a man is both separate and foreign; what comes out of a man has been born from within.

And with that final change, God has declared our menu to be wide open. According to the Bible, a Christian should have no trepidation in consuming an animal. This fact was confirmed to Peter in Acts 10, when he received a vision from God declaring all foods to be clean. It was further approved in the writings of Paul, which we see in detail in Romans 14. It also is not lost on me that Jesus is directly responsible for catching—and therefore, killing—at least 153 fish during His lifetime. (You can see John 21:11 for the rest of that story.)

—

What goes into a man is both separate and foreign; what comes out of a man has been born from within.

—

My point here is not to debate the morality of meat eating, but rather, to highlight how our diet has changed over time. We started as vegetarians, and then, meat was added. The menu is wide open for Christians today. It does appear, however, that we will see a reversion to greenery by the end of our story. (Warning: If you are a lover of burgers and bratwurst, if you believe that bacon is best served at all times of the day, then you might want to brace yourself before this next section.)

OUR HEAVENLY DIET

Based on what the Bible tells us, our meats will eventually be pulled from the menu. How can we know this? This can first be discerned through the words of Isaiah, who foretold some changes to the animal kingdom. It appears that even the food chain will be redeemed by the saving work of Christ. These are God's words about animals in heaven:

> For behold, I create new heavens and a new earth; and the former things will not be remembered or come to mind . . . The wolf and the lamb will graze together, and the lion will eat straw like the ox. (Isaiah 65:17, 25 NASB)

Take notice of God's vocabulary here. When was the last time that you saw a wolf graze? And how often have you seen a lion eat straw? Never. And why? Because wolves do not graze; they hunt! Lions do not eat straw; they eat living flesh! But in the new heavens and new earth, neither the wolf nor the lion will eat other animals. They will return to their original diets of Eden (Genesis 1:30). Therefore, if the wolf and lion will become vegetarians, it is not a stretch to assume that we humans will also. As Randy Alcorn writes:

> We're told animals' eating habits will change—why not ours? The food chain may seem natural to us, but I believe it violates God's original design. No more curse and death means no more food chain involving living creatures As radical a shift as that may seem, it will likely be a return to God's original design.[39]

In the book of Revelation, John further explains this shift to our origins. He says that the new earth will be a place where "death shall be no more, neither shall there be mourning, nor crying, nor pain anymore, for the former things have passed away" (Revelation 21:4). You will notice that John provides no specifications on the type of death or the type of pain that is being eradicated. Rather, he speaks of death and pain in a general sense. He does not say that only human death will be erased; he also leaves room for the animal kingdom.

But if no animal dies, then how can we eat meat?

Exactly.

Because of the "lack of death" clause in this new earth prophecy, it appears that our diet will return back to greens. The curse will be gone, and with it, all death. Our diet will return to the diet of Eden.

So, just to recap, here is a visual depiction of man's diet throughout history:

Era	Diet	Key Verse(s)
Garden of Eden	Fruits, vegetables, nuts, and seeds	Genesis 1:29
Post-flood	Fruits, vegetables, nuts, and seeds, with the addition of animal meat	Genesis 9:3
The Mosaic Covenant	God creates a special diet for the nation of Israel, banning them from eating certain foods from the post-flood diet (e.g., no pork, shellfish, mice, and so on).	Leviticus 11, Deuteronomy 14
Ministry of Jesus	Jesus declares all foods to be clean for the nation of Israel.	Mark 7:18–19
Church Age (present day)	God reaffirms that all foods—and all people—are clean in His sight.	Acts 10, Romans 14
New Earth (the future)	A reversion back to our pre-sin diet, consisting of fruits, vegetables, nuts, and seeds	Isaiah 65, Revelation 21:4

Soul Food

You might be wondering why any of this matters. What can we learn from the history of food? For one thing, we can learn that man has always had a diet, and that diet has been dictated by God. But the second point is even more personal, and it was my reason for writing this chapter.

We often take food for granted. Calories in, calories out. If we want to slim down, we start counting our macros. If we have a bad day, we reach for the ice cream. But so many of us miss out on the blessing of food, thus leaving some joy on the table. Food is yet another way that God draws us closer. It is a way that He strengthens our relationship with Him. God could have made us like plants or trees—or Superman, for that matter—and allowed us to absorb our energy from the sun. But He didn't do that. No. God loves us much more than plants or Superman, so He has given us a greater blessing. He has chosen to bless us above all life forms.

Human beings were the only creation made in God's image. The dolphins were not, and the angels were not. We are, quite literally, God's favorite creatures. We are His children. It is for this reason that we enjoy the best of God's blessings—the best intelligence, the best sex lives, the best forgiveness from God, the best access to God, and yes, even the best culinary experience. The monkey eats bananas, the shark eats fish, but we, as humans, enjoy both. We eat hot food and cold food, plant food and meat food. Our God has given us the choice. While a shark eats his fish as a matter of instinct, the human's experience of food is different. A human has the ability to pause, reflect, and give thanks for his food. He can recognize the Chef who has fed him his meal. As the psalmist once wrote of the Master Chef:

> He causes the grass to grow for the cattle,
> And vegetation for the service of man,
> That he may bring forth food from the earth,

And wine that makes glad the heart of man,
Oil to make his face shine,
And bread which strengthens man's heart.
(Psalm 104:14–15 NKJV)

God gives us our food to bless us. He gives us our food to draw us close. Eating can be, in the truest sense of the word, an act of worship for the Christian. Tell me, when you have found yourself in deep moments of worship—perhaps accompanied by music or alone in nature—did your heart not cry out with unspeakable gladness? Is worship not merely our joy spilling over? *Thank You! Thank You! Thank You!* we say. If we are filled with joy at the prompting of music, then why does a meal have to be any different? Why not experience this joy at least three times each day? As Fred Bahnson writes:

> Food is not a product. It is not "fuel for the machine." It is not a commodity or a reflection of our technological ingenuity. It is before everything else an unearned gift from God, manna from heaven, a blessing.[40]

It is 9:00 a.m. in the morning as I write these words. With all of this talk of food, I am thinking ahead to my dinner tonight. My friends and I are going to our favorite Thai place. Will I order the pad thai? Maybe the pad kra pao? At this point in time, all I can know for sure is this: When I sit down for dinner with my friends, and I have that warm, delicious, sweet, spicy, beautiful blessing before me, it will help me draw closer to God. No longer will I take my food for granted, as each meal is a moment to thank Him.

God gives us our food to pull us close.

Now pull up a chair and feast.

Today's Challenge

Schedule (or cook) your favorite meal.

With every step of the process, let your thoughts go to Jesus and your gratitude for Him. When your food is delicious and brings comfort and pleasure, that was His idea in the first place.

And then, for the easy part: Enjoy your meal!

YOUR SEXUALITY

*Do you not know that your bodies are temples of the Holy Spirit, who
is in you, whom you have received from God? You are not your own;
you were bought at a price. Therefore honor God with your bodies.*
—1 CORINTHIANS 6:19–20 NIV

As unmarried Christians, the Bible leaves no room for our
sexual activity. But despite the clear commands that we find
in God's Word, we still have to contend with our sexual
urges. The question, then, remains: *How should single Christians treat
their sexuality?*

There are a number of ways we can misuse our bodies, and this
chapter will talk about three. First, we will discuss the damaging effects
of "purity culture." Second, we will discuss sex out of wedlock and a
cure for fornication. Third, and finally, we will discuss the increasingly
popular—yet biblically outlawed—practice of homosexuality. We have
plenty to discuss, so let's dive right in. First, a discussion on purity.

PURITY CULTURE

I do not wish to vilify sexual purity. I want to be clear about that from the beginning. To abstain from sex outside of marriage is God's will for all of our lives. As it says in the book of Hebrews, "Let marriage be held in honor among all, and let the marriage bed be undefiled, for God will judge the sexually immoral and adulterous" (Hebrews 13:4). But despite purity being a good ideal, the church has mishandled it in a number of ways. Just like too much water (or sunlight) can make someone ill, too much focus on purity has negative consequences.

The 1990s and 2000s ushered in a strong overemphasis on purity. This movement among Christian circles was eventually labeled the "purity culture." A host of ministries emerged during this time, with "True Love Waits" and the "Silver Ring Thing" being named among the most popular.[41] These ministries were also the purveyors of "purity rings," which were outward expressions of one's commitment to chastity.

Many books on purity were written as well, with the most notable being *I Kissed Dating Goodbye* by Joshua Harris. In that blockbuster bestseller, Harris encouraged his readers toward a highly intentional form of dating. While few people can balk at intentionality, his book also created a wave of intensity. What originally started with great intentions soon drifted away from the gospel. In the throes of the purity culture, young Christians became so busy "guarding their heart" and "waiting for marriage" that they forgot about their joy in our Savior. Conversing with the opposite sex became far too intense, and marriage—not heaven—was the prize.

But there was another unforeseen consequence of purity culture. There is now a community of women (and perhaps even men) who have trouble with sex in their marriages. Some have even had trouble consummating their wedding night. Their sexual deterrent is rarely physical; it is almost always psychological. Because they have been telling themselves "sex is bad" for so long, they have wired their bodies to feel shame around sex. As a result, they shudder at the thought of having sex with their spouses, and a blessing is spoiled by lies.

For the single Christian, the proper thinking about sex is not, "Sex is bad," but rather, "Sex is great, a wonderful gift, and I will enjoy it whenever God wants me to." Let's remember: God made sex pleasurable to bless His children. His intent for sex has always been good. In fact, it is God Himself who tells young husbands:

> Let your fountain be blessed, and rejoice in the wife of your youth, a lovely deer, a graceful doe. Let her breasts fill you at all times with delight; be intoxicated always in her love. (Proverbs 5:18–19)

The point to remember about purity is this: Our righteousness, our chastity, any shameless joys that tomorrow may bring, these all can be found in the person of Christ. It is Christ—not a celibate path to the altar—that is our righteousness. Christ is our purity. Christ is our joy. This does not somehow negate our call to obey God's commandments, but it does put our efforts into proper perspective. The single Christian knows the truth of the matter: Sex is not bad; it is simply not yet.

It is Christ—not a celibate path to the altar—that is our righteousness.

FORNICATION

The biblical call to abstinence is obvious. The church remains essentially unanimous on this issue. And yet, despite nearly total agreement within the church, many Christians still engage in fornication today. Our men are driven by lust and passion, and our women offer sex as a means of exchange. While some women are tempted by the pleasures of sex, many others use sex as relational currency. They hope that in giving their bodies to a boyfriend or fiancé, then that man will love them—and stay with them—forever. Many hopes have turned out to be miscalculations.

Nevertheless, the Bible has plenty to say about sex outside of marriage. It tells us exactly how to cope with our sexual urges. As the apostle Paul once wrote:

> It is God's will that you should be sanctified: that you should avoid sexual immorality; that each of you should learn to control your own body in a way that is holy and honorable, not in passionate lust like the pagans, who do not know God; and that in this matter no one should wrong or take advantage of a brother or sister. The Lord will punish all those who commit such sins. (1 Thessalonians 4:3–6 NIV)

The children of God are supposed to be holy, and sex outside of marriage is an unholy act. To be holy means to be "set apart," so the holy person should be—in his very nature—different, abnormal, and, in some cases, weird. Having sex outside of marriage is common; waiting for sex within marriage is uncommon. That is the point. The only way to be holy is to be different from the crowd, and one way that Christians are holy is through their sexuality. The apostle Paul told young men to treat young women "as sisters, with absolute purity" (1 Timothy 5:2 NIV). He also told them to "treat the parts of your earthly body as dead to sexual immorality" (Colossians 3:5 NASB).

But for as much as Paul wrote about sexual purity, he was also a realist on the human condition. He knew that sexual temptations are still strong for the Christian, so he left us clear instructions for combatting them. Here is what Paul wrote to the Christians of Corinth:

Now regarding the questions you asked in your letter. Yes, it is good to abstain from sexual relations. But because there is so much sexual immorality, each man should have his own wife, and each woman should have her own husband. The husband should fulfill his wife's sexual needs, and the wife should fulfill her husband's needs. The wife gives authority over her body to her husband, and the husband gives authority over his body to his wife. Do not deprive each other of sexual relations, unless you both agree to refrain from sexual intimacy for a limited time so you can give yourselves more completely to prayer. (1 Corinthians 7:1–5 NLT)

While Paul does not explicitly mention what was asked in their "questions," it is obvious that the Corinthians were struggling with fornication. According to Paul, there was "so much sexual immorality" among them that they wrote to seek his opinion. They wondered how to contend with their sexual urges. And what did Paul say? What was his prescription for controlling their lusts?

Marriage.

That's right, marriage. Paul said that if they were burning with passion that they could not control, then they should seek out a spouse and get married. He did not tell them to find a distraction, a hobby, or a twelve-step program. He told them to find a spouse. *Each man should have his own wife*, he said. *Each woman should have her own husband.* Instead of living a promiscuous lifestyle with multiple partners, Paul told the Corinthians to settle down.

If, by chance, you find yourself burning with sexual cravings, if your uncontrolled urges have led you to pornography, then you might need to get more serious about marriage. I say that not as a criticism. I say it to encourage you. You, my friend, might just need a spouse. Every time you slip, every time you engage with pornography, that might be a simple, real-world reminder that God has designed you to

—

One man, one woman,

in marriage, often.

—

be married. While we are certainly commanded to master our urges, Paul's words are pointing us to our one approved outlet. *The husband should fulfill his wife's sexual needs, and the wife shall fulfill her husband's needs* (1 Corinthians 7:3). Perhaps the sin of fornication (with others) or masturbation (with yourself) has allowed you to sidestep the altar. But no more. It is our desire for intimacy, our itching for sex, that can actually push us toward marriage. There is nothing wrong with having this motivation. Paul offers us only two choices when it comes to our sexuality. We can either be married and fulfilled by our spouse, or we can be happily single and in control of our bodies.

Here is the biblical mandate for sex:

One man, one woman, in marriage, often.

Anything outside these parameters is evil and devilish, and it ultimately leads to our hurt. But there is still another way we can misuse our bodies, and one that God describes as detestable.

HOMOSEXUALITY

The conversation around homosexuality has become increasingly emotional. Perhaps you have noticed. In fact, you might even be surprised that I would bring up this subject. Nevertheless, the Bible tells us to expose false teachings, false teachers, and false doctrines, and thus, a discussion on the topic is warranted.

What once was unequivocally denounced by the church—and America as a whole, I might add—is now being accepted by Christians en masse. But despite what secular culture might tell you, the Bible is perfectly clear on homosexuality. It calls it a sin every time it's addressed. The practice of homosexuality is just as terrible—or trivial—as lying, cheating, or stealing. While homosexuality is not the gravest of all sins, we still need to be honest and call it what it is—a sin. In fact, there are five specific passages in the Bible where God explicitly condemns homosexuality. Here are those five passages in their order of appearance:

1. You shall not sleep with a male as one sleeps with a female; it is an abomination. (Leviticus 18:22 NASB)

2. If a man has sexual relations with a man as one does with a woman, both of them have done what is detestable. They are to be put to death; their blood will be on their own heads. (Leviticus 20:13 NIV)

3. For this reason God gave them over to degrading passions; for their women exchanged natural relations for that which is contrary to nature, and likewise the men, too, abandoned natural relations with women and burned in their desire toward one another, males with males committing shameful acts and receiving in their own persons the due penalty of their error. (Romans 1:26–27 NASB)

4. Do not be deceived; neither the sexually immoral, nor idolaters, nor adulterers, nor homosexuals, nor thieves, nor the greedy, nor those habitually drunk, nor verbal abusers, nor swindlers, will inherit the kingdom of God. (1 Corinthians 6:9–10 NASB)

5. We also know that the law is made not for the righteous but for lawbreakers and rebels, the ungodly and sinful, the unholy and irreligious, for those who kill their fathers or mothers, for murderers, for the sexually immoral, for those

practicing homosexuality, for slave traders and liars and perjur-
ers—and for whatever else is contrary to the sound doctrine.
(1 Timothy 1:9–10 NIV)

Just to be clear, that statement in Leviticus 20:13 (the second
passage above) is not binding on us today. Issuing the death penalty for homosexuality was an old covenant punishment for Old
Testament Israel. In that day and age, God also imposed the death
penalty on adulterers (Leviticus 20:10), those who cursed their parents
(Exodus 21:17), sorcerers (Exodus 22:18), those who worked on the
Sabbath (Exodus 35:2), and many others.

Needless to say, while the expedience of God's judgment has
changed over time, His morality and character have not. Unless God
explicitly states that He is changing His commands on a subject—like
He did with the Sabbath day or the dietary food laws—then we have
to assume that His stance is unchanged. Therefore, when reading these
five passages about homosexuality—found in both the Old Testament
and New Testament alike—we see an obvious theme put forward
by God. Notice the words that God uses to describe homosexuality.
Abomination. Detestable. Degrading. Shameful. He calls it "ungodly"
and "contrary to sound doctrine."

It also is not lost on me that God compares homosexuality to
some painfully obvious sins—things like idolatry, adultery, slave
trading, and murder. The Holy Spirit, in His infinite foresight and
wisdom, undoubtedly predicted the church's backsliding on this
issue. But because of the passages in 1 Corinthians and 1 Timothy,
the Christian's beliefs are necessarily conditional. There are biblical
guardrails wherein we must stay. For example, let's say that we run into
a churchgoer who says homosexuality is allowed by God. More often
than not, that person will say something like "We all are sinners!" or
"A sin is a sin!" Both of those things are perfectly true, but because
of Paul's words in 1 Corinthians and 1 Timothy, we cannot permit

one sin while forbidding another. In other words, if someone believes that God condones *homosexuality*, then they also must believe that God condones *murder*. The Spirit leaves no room for personal biases.

Therefore, if you tell a homosexual that God loves them "just as they are," then you must also be willing to say that to a murderer. "God loves you, Mr. Murderer, *just as you are*." I have yet to meet anyone who would make such a statement. If a murderer refuses to change his ways, our society will shun him as evil; if a murderer announces he's become homosexual, our society will throw a parade.

The truth is, God does not love any of us "just as we are." That is a half-baked statement that leads many astray. It actually pushes people *away* from Jesus. When someone says that God loves us "just as" we are, what they really mean is that God loves us "in spite of" who we are. That is the more accurate use of language. The reality is, God loves us enough to *ignore* who we are—the dirty, wretched rebels who spurn Him. It is only through the blood of Jesus that God can love us, forgive us, and make us clean. That is the entire point of the gospel! Despite the obvious sinners that you and I are, God sees us for what we can be through Jesus. He adopts us as sons and makes us clean.

At this point, you might be wondering, *But can't you be Christian and homosexual? Isn't it possible for someone to be both?*

The short answer is no. No, you cannot.

While a Christian can certainly be tempted by homosexual urges—just like a Christian could be tempted to fornicate, watch pornography, or lust—it is taking the action that makes one disobedient. Therefore, the very term "homosexual Christian" is an oxymoron. When a person willingly, consistently disobeys Christ, that person is simply not a follower of Christ. Like oil and water (or silence and noise), the Bible describes

When a person willingly, consistently disobeys Christ, that person is simply not a follower of Christ.

Christians and homosexuals with complete exclusivity. You are one or the other, but you cannot be both. It was Jesus Himself who said, "If you love Me, you will keep My commandments" (John 14:15). As we have seen from the five passages above, the Bible's stance on the subject is clear.

If we truly care about those who are practicing homosexuality, we must present them with Scripture and then let them decide. While the Christian is not called to "parent" a stranger, we are still called to make disciples and share the truths of the Bible. More often than not, the average Christian will try to be overly kind to someone who is practicing homosexuality. No one can blame them for that. Their kindness is warranted, but their message is wrong. It is always the same:

Grace, grace, grace upon grace.

It is all grace and no truth. All love, but no rod. No changes. No repentance. No feathers ruffled! Their goal is accomplished (in keeping their friendship), but their mission has failed (because their friend is still hell-bound). Extending more grace than God is a dangerous game.

So, if you find yourself living a homosexual lifestyle, let me encourage you with this truth: All Christians—no matter our relationship status or sexual preference—are called to offer our bodies to God. *All of us.* We are told to treat our bodies as "living sacrifices" (Romans 12:1). In doing this, we choose the will of God over our momentary urges. That is the contract we have made with our God. For some, this will mean resisting the urge to have sex out of wedlock; for others, it will mean walking away from homosexuality. And then, as we continue to obey the commands of the Bible, God will progressively renew our minds in the process. He will change our urges and give us power to master them.

God takes worldly creatures and makes them saints.

He takes the "normal" and "common" and makes them holy.

FINAL THOUGHTS

God's will for sex is pretty straightforward. It is a wonderful gift that He intends for His children. Men marry women, and women marry men. Men sleep with women, and women sleep with men. It is that simple. Sex is certainly a blessing that should be enjoyed, but it is made for a select group of people and at God's chosen time. To the single-minded Christian who is wired for sex, remember this in your season of waiting:

Sex is not bad; it is simply not yet.

You'll enjoy it whenever God wants you to.

TODAY'S CHALLENGE

List some common thoughts that you have about sex. Reconcile those beliefs with the truths of the Bible.

Which of your beliefs about sex are true? Which of your beliefs about sex are false?

Sex is

- _____ (True)(False)
- _____ (True)(False)
- _____ (True)(False)
- _____ (True)(False)
- _____ (True)(False)

DAY TWENTY-NINE

YOUR DEATH

For to me to live is Christ, and to die is gain.
—PHILIPPIANS 1:21

Death is often our greatest fear. Sure, we might be frightened by heights, crowds, or the occasional spider, but deep down, the truest fear of a human is death. We tremble at the thought of everything ending. What happens on the day when all goes black? The Christian, however, does not harbor such fear. In fact, the Christian can feel the opposite way—he can actually look forward to death.

A STRUGGLE WITH SADNESS

In my mid-twenties, I went through a significant season of loss. It felt like a "mid-twenties crisis," if there ever was such a thing. While I did grow up in a Christian home and always believed that I was a Christian, I officially submitted my life to the Lord at age twenty-five. That was when I decided to go even deeper. *Here's my life, Lord.* What I did not expect, however, was that after I submitted my life to God, I often struggled with feeling sad. I am not saying that I felt sad *a lot*, but rather, that I mentally wrestled with the fact of my sadness. I felt as if I should not be sad, like a more mature Christian might not feel that way. It felt wrong, weak, and immature. Even unholy. *Christians are happy all the time* was the lie I would hear in my head.

But that changed one Sunday while I was sitting in church. The pastor was teaching on John 6. Truth be told, I did not pay much attention to his words that day. I can vaguely recall him quoting Jesus' words, "I am the bread of life," but my mind was adrift after that. Frankly, I was more concerned with my personal worries—an imminent home purchase, my seemingly endless work responsibilities, the hint of fear that I'd never be married, and so on. Life felt hard, and I could not see a path of escape.

But then, we worshipped. The congregation stood up, we lifted our hands, and we praised our Lord in song. My mind was still wandering a bit, but I played along with the crowd. Eventually, I found myself dreaming of a place that did not feel hard. I longed for a life that was different, where everything was calm, easy, and peaceful, where there were no deadlines, stresses, or gaps in my heart. It was then, on that Sunday, for the very first time, that I finally realized this truth:

We need not be fearful of death.

In a sense, our death and departure might be what we're longing for. I understand how those words could sound a bit morbid, so please know that is not my intention. In reality, it is not *death* or *dying* that our hearts are longing for; we are really just longing for heaven.

To Live Is Christ, To Die Is Gain

The most obvious example of this "longing for heaven" comes from the apostle Paul's letter to Philippi. The overwhelming consensus is that Paul wrote that letter while imprisoned in the city of Rome. In the first chapter of that epistle, Paul writes:

> Now I want you to know, brothers and sisters, that my circumstances have turned out for the greater progress of the gospel, so that my imprisonment in the cause of Christ has become well known throughout the praetorian guard and to everyone else, and that most of the brothers and sisters, trusting in the Lord because of my imprisonment, have far more courage to speak the word of God without fear. (Philippians 1:12–14 NASB)

Just to recap: Paul was imprisoned because of his faith, everyone around him knew it, and other Christians were emboldened because of that fact. He also mentioned that the praetorian guard and "everyone else" was moved by his presence. Even the Romans saw something different in Paul. In that sense, Paul's imprisonment was not all bad—it was actually quite good and purposeful. It was God's mission for him in that day and age. Paul continued by saying:

> I also will rejoice, for I know that this will turn out for my deliverance through your prayers and the provision of the Spirit of Jesus Christ, according to my eager expectation and hope, that I will not be put to shame in anything, but that with all boldness, Christ will even now, as always, be exalted in my body, whether by life or by death. (Philippians 1:18–20 NASB)

Despite being in prison, Paul still had unwavering hope of being set free. Either his distress would be ended by being set free, or his distress would be ended through corporal punishment. And notice how Paul considers both of these paths to be positive outcomes! *By life or by death*, he writes. This is obviously quite a radical claim, but Paul explained just why he felt that way:

> For to me, to live is Christ, and to die is gain. But if I am to live on in the flesh, this will mean fruitful labor for me; and

I do not know which to choose. But I am hard-pressed from both directions, having the desire to depart and be with Christ, for that is very much better; yet to remain on in the flesh is more necessary for your sakes. (Philippians 1:21–24 NASB)

Why does Paul rejoice at the thought of death? The answer is simply this: On the day that he died, he would be with Christ. In Paul's estimation, the thought of walking with Jesus forever was *far better, very much better* (NASB), or, as one translation puts it, *far better indeed* (BSB) than anything this world had to offer. If there was ever a Christian who connected with God, it was Paul. And yet, despite his great and unparalleled access to Christ on earth, he still wanted to die and be with Him in person. Selfishly speaking, Paul knew that his experience of Jesus was less than it could be as long as he stayed on the earth. He knew there was more to be had.

But Paul was willing to stay if he had to. In fact, he told his readers that he was torn between his two options: either leaving his body to be with Christ (his preference) or staying on earth for the sake of the gospel. This is why Paul so famously said, "To live is Christ, and to die is gain." For Paul to continue living on in the body—despite his selfish desire to die and leave—would be to serve in a way as Jesus Christ did. Just as Jesus had done before him, Paul was willing to sacrifice his time and pleasure for the benefit of others. Paul was willing to stay to rescue the lost.

It is at this point, however, that some Christians get uneasy at the words of Paul. To some, it can feel unspiritual or ungodly to look forward to death. *Very much better to depart and die? Who ever would say such a thing?* they ask.

> *In Paul's estimation, the thought of walking with Jesus forever was far better, very much better (NASB), or, far better indeed (BSB) than anything this world had to offer.*

Jesus was raised from the dead and our sins are erased, so we have full access to God, right now!

In a sense, I can understand their heart behind this. I do. But on the other side of the coin, we must ignore a litany of Scripture to reach their conclusion. The biblical view is clear on this issue. Over and over again—no matter what the reader wants or feels—the Bible points our eyes toward heaven. It tells us that, in fact, we do *not* have the full experience of God right now. For example, notice what Paul wrote to the Christians at Corinth:

> For we know in part and we prophesy in part, but when the perfect comes, the partial will pass away. When I was a child, I spoke like a child, I thought like a child, I reasoned like a child. When I became a man, I gave up childish ways. For now we see in a mirror dimly, but then face to face. Now I know in part; then I shall know fully, even as I have been fully known. (1 Corinthians 13:9–12)

How does Paul describe our current reality? He uses words like *partial*, *childish*, and *dimly* to explain it. Our experience of Jesus is less than complete. Paul uses a threefold metaphor to describe our scenario:

Now, we think like children. Then, we will think like adults.

Now, we see through a clouded mirror. Then, we will see face-to-face.

Now, we know our God in part. Then, we will know our God in full.

The childish mind, once matured, can behold and appreciate more. In that sense, Paul is actually describing *himself* as a child in 1 Corinthians 13:11. As long as Paul continued to walk the earth, he could only see in part and prophesy in part; but once Paul died, he would finally know God in full.

Now, we know our God in part. Then, we will know our God in full.

HOPE IN HEAVEN

I danced around my fears, insecurities, and longings for years. I was looking for some sort of answer on earth. While I intuitively knew that money, sex, or anything else could never deliver my paradise, I hoped that at least Jesus could. I hoped that if I became "Christian" enough, if I prayed and fasted and sought Jesus enough, then my sadness and longings would vanish.

But I was wrong.

Dead wrong.

The longings and yearnings were here to stay.

Even after I gave God my heart, my angst refused to leave me. This was when my "struggle with sadness" began to emerge. But what I realize now is that I had not missed anything. I was simply experiencing the groanings of Paul. In reality, it is natural for the Christian to feel some sadness, but that sadness is also coupled with hope. Our hearts can groan to be with Jesus, but they should also be filled with great expectation. One day, someday, we will actually be with our Lord.

Here is the freeing reality that I came to in worship: As long as we live on earth, we will *never* have Jesus as much as we want to. This is the message that Paul wrote in his letters, and it is exactly the reason why death can be gain. This is also why the apostle John could say, "Come, Lord Jesus!" on the very last page of the Bible (Revelation 22:20). You will notice that he didn't say, "*Stay*, Lord Jesus." And just for context, this was the very same John who was there, in person, when the resurrected Jesus had promised, "And surely I am with you always, to the very end of the age" (Matthew 28:20 NIV).

It is natural for the Christian to feel some sadness, but that sadness is also coupled with hope.

Had John forgotten these words of Jesus?

Why ask Jesus to "come" if He had promised to stay?

Here's the catch: While Jesus was promising to remain with His disciples, He was only ever promising to be with them in spirit. Jesus was "with" the disciples just like He is with you or me right now. Therefore, when John said, "Come, Lord Jesus," he was doing so because he wanted to have Jesus in the flesh! He wanted to walk with his Lord, face-to-face, man to Man, as he had done before in the past.

Today, you and I experience Jesus dimly, just as Paul and John did before us. But then, one day, when we finally die, we will see Him with our very eyes. It was only once I gave myself permission to believe this that my joy was able to blossom. It was okay to feel sad. It was okay to groan. It was even okay to no longer fear death. It is only once we cast our longings to heaven that our hope will be properly placed.

The Spirit-filled Christian has no need to fear death.

On the day that he dies, he lives.

Today's Challenge

Answer the following questions:

How do you want to view your life in light of Jesus's return?

_____

_____

_____

_____

What do you most look forward to when thinking about seeing Jesus?

_____

_____

_____

_____

YOUR FUTURE

"For I know the plans I have for you," declares the LORD, "plans to prosper
you and not to harm you, plans to give you hope and a future."
—JEREMIAH 29:11 NIV

I read from Matthew 6 this morning. We call this portion of Scripture the Sermon on the Mount. It is where Jesus institutes the Lord's prayer, as well as some wisdom on wealth and worry. I must admit, I have been feeling quite worried these days. I worry about turning thirty-four next year. I worry that I'm destined to be single forever. I worry that I always will feel this lonely—and there is nothing more crippling than loneliness. I worry that even if I do get married—at fifty years old, I presume—then my wife will likely be of the same age, and thus, we won't be able to have our own children. I still do my best to trust in God, but even so, I worry.

The first thing that struck me in Matthew 6 was that Jesus did not pray for the future. He seemed only concerned with the here and now. "Give us this day our daily bread," was His prayer for provision from God (Matthew 6:11). He did not ask for bread next week, next month, or next year. He simply asked for God to feed Him today. Jesus further emphasized this point just a few verses later when He said, "So

> *So do not worry about tomorrow; for tomorrow will care for itself.*
>
> — MATTHEW 6:34 NASB

do not worry about tomorrow; for tomorrow will care for itself. Each day has enough trouble of its own" (Matthew 6:34 NASB).

Those words challenged me a lot. *Do not worry about tomorrow.* As I considered my worries in greater detail, nearly all of them had to do with the distant future. I was worried about things that I could not control. But what if I stopped and listened to Jesus? What if I narrowed my focus and prayed for today? For one, my life would certainly be simpler. That much sounded nice. But then again, if I surrendered my future to God, that would also require me to surrender control. I did not like that part as much. After all, if I did not worry about tomorrow, next week, or ten years from now, then how on earth would my life hold together? Who else would ensure that my plan was fulfilled?

I know that these questions are foolish and selfish, but the sin living in us can sound so convincing. The truth is, it was time for me to admit that I was deeply afraid. I was afraid to surrender my future to God, knowing He might lay out a path that I would not have chosen.

What if God had decided that I'd be single forever?

What if *God* was the light at the end of this tunnel?

OUR LIVING HOPE

While our future might seem to be so unsure, we can know that God's plan is perfectly sure. Perhaps that is why He makes us wait. By delaying—or denying—our plans for the future, God gives us the space to consider His own. Our plans are for earth; His plans are for heaven. Our plans are for now; His plans are forever. But this process of waiting does not leave us empty-handed. By forgetting ourselves, our goals, and our plans for the future, we are all the more able to receive greater gifts. God certainly desires to give us good things, but we need to be taught how to seek gifts that last. In the words of the apostle Peter:

Our plans are for earth; His plans are for heaven. Our plans are for now; His plans are forever.

> Blessed be the God and Father of our Lord Jesus Christ, who according to His great mercy has caused us to be born again to a living hope through the resurrection of Jesus Christ from the dead, to obtain an inheritance which is imperishable, undefiled, and will not fade away, reserved in heaven for you, who are protected by the power of God through faith for a salvation ready to be revealed in the last time. In this you greatly rejoice, even though now for a little while, if necessary, you have been distressed by various trials, so that the proof of your faith, being more precious than gold which perishes though tested by fire, may be found to result in praise, glory, and honor at the revelation of Jesus Christ; and though you have not seen Him, you love Him, and though you do not see Him now, but believe in Him, you greatly rejoice with joy inexpressible and full of glory, obtaining as the outcome of your faith, the salvation of your souls. (1 Peter 1:3–9 NASB)

So then, what do we receive because of our faith? What are God's lasting gifts that will pass through the fire? They are not paychecks, promotions, or seasonal comforts. Our faith in Jesus gives us much more than that. His gifts include:

- A living hope (v. 3)
- An inheritance that is imperishable, undefiled, and unfading (v. 4)

- An inheritance that is reserved in heaven (v. 4)
- Protection by God (v. 5)
- Rejoicing, despite trials (v. 6)
- Praise, glory, and honor (v. 7)
- A love for Jesus, without seeing Him (v. 8)
- Rejoicing, inexpressible joy, and glory (v. 8)
- The salvation of our souls (v. 9)

This is why the Christian can have hope *today*. By having a relationship with Jesus Christ, we can unlock the mystery and delight in God's promises. It is with this knowledge, this hope, that we can face the trials of today with courage. We can know that our earthly trials will end. Instead, we hope in the One who *is* our future—the powerful, wonderful King of heaven. As the apostle Peter once told his readers, "Therefore, prepare your minds for action, keep sober in spirit, set your hope completely on the grace to be brought to you at the revelation of Jesus Christ" (1 Peter 1:13 NASB). When our eyes are truly fixed on Jesus, our future is bright, indeed.

THE PAULINE ADVANTAGE

Our journey together is coming to an end. I hope that these last thirty days have been fruitful for you, and it has been my pleasure to walk this road with you. As we conclude our time together, we will finish our journey in the place we began. Let us turn our attention back to Dietrich Bonhoeffer, that puzzling, pious, pastoring German.

On April 5, 1943, Bonhoeffer was arrested by the Gestapo and sent to prison. The Nazis ripped him away from his work, his family, and his fiancé, Maria. Maria and Dietrich would never be married. They would never consummate, procreate, or grow old together.

For nearly eighteen months, Bonhoeffer lived in Cell 92 of Tegel Prison, still mostly unaware of what he'd been charged. One can only imagine how lonely he was. There was nothing but time for his unceasing mind. Oddly enough, many of Bonhoeffer's best writings were penned in that cell, including a portion of his magnum opus, *Ethics*, his *Letters and Papers from Prison,* and more. But despite his voluminous writing habits, this imprisoned Christian still had many fears. In his now famous poem, *Who Am I?*, Bonhoeffer shed some light on his unending questions:

> Who am I? This or the other?
> Am I one person today and tomorrow another?
> Am I both at once? A hypocrite before others,
> And before myself a contemptibly woebegone weakling?
> Or is something within me still like a beaten army,
> Fleeing in disorder from victory already achieved?
> Who am I? They mock me, these lonely questions of mine.
> Whoever I am, Thou knowest, O God, I am Thine![42]

It would be easy for us to look at Bonhoeffer, Peter, or the apostle Paul and assume that they never had doubts. But they did. They certainly did. While these men might have been saints, they also were humans, all fully endowed with the virus called sin. But why would we flee if we are the victors? How can we fret if our future is sure? Peter knew that, Paul knew that, and the inmate in Cell 92 knew that. But this "knowing" and "hoping" does not shield us from hardships. History tells us that Paul was beheaded in the city of Rome.[43] Peter was crucified upside down.[44] And then, on the morning of April 9, 1945, Bonhoeffer was hanged in the city of Flossenbürg.[45] Despite all of his piety and all of his prayers, God did not choose to spare Dietrich Bonhoeffer. His body was burned in a pile of corpses.

I think many of us refuse to go all in on God out of fear of the sacrifice required. Would you want to trade places with Peter or Paul? But then again, there is something innately human, something deep inside of us, that understands the goodness of personal sacrifice. It is selfish and cowardly to keep for ourselves, but it is good and right to give of ourselves.

You, my friend, are single for a reason. God has granted you this season for a specific purpose. You have the very same advantage as the apostle Paul, as have many single Christians throughout church history. The only question remaining to ask is this:

Are you ready to seize your advantage?

But what of my plans? your mind may argue. *And what of the future? What if God wants me to be single forever? Or what if I'm martyred? What if I'm imprisoned? What if I face the most horrible suffering? Will I really go spouseless and childless for life? Am I destined to decades of living alone?*

Pause.

Breathe.

Put your trust in the One who has written your story.

Just like the great Dietrich Bonhoeffer before us, we are going to have questions about our future. We are going to have fears, and we are going to have doubts. That is okay. The good news is, it is not our job to "figure it out." Our future is written, and our fate is secure. God loves us, He is for us, and He holds the pen. Our God is the Master of holy surprises.

With that truth in mind, let us cry to our King—Lord Jesus, divine: Whoever I am, Thou knowest, O God, I am Thine!

TODAY'S CHALLENGE

The moment of commitment.

If you have not done so already—and you have considered the costs (and benefits) of this decision—I invite you to give your life to Jesus. Right here, right now. If you are prepared to take this step of faith, use this moment for private prayer. Invite Jesus into your heart, completely and officially, and surrender your life to the Lord.

If, however, you have already committed your life to Jesus, then I still have a challenge for you. I encourage you, my fellow believer, to take this moment to go even deeper. Are you prepared to give Jesus *more* of yourself? Are you prepared to give Jesus *all* of yourself? How about your hopes, your dreams, your plans, and your future? It is human nature to hold onto these things; it is God's invitation to surrender these things.

Go deeper. Trust Him. He is your living hope.

ACKNOWLEDGMENTS

To the team at Streamline Books: We did it! Thank you to Alex Demczak, Annika Bergen, Becca Blackburn, Abigael Elliott, Ginny Glass, Chloie Benton, Dave Sheets, and everyone else who impacted this project. I could not have done it without your help, and I am so grateful for your work and encouragement.

To Rory and AJ Vaden and my teammates at Brand Builders Group: Thank you for empowering the "mission-driven messenger" to make this world a better place. Your guidance and expertise have shortened my learning curve by years—perhaps even a decade. Thank you for showing me the way!

To my Bible study: Willie Shaw, Shane Lantigua, Wesley Purcell, Sam Wilson, Jonathan Lutz, and Alex Macinnis—Iron sharpens iron. Thank you for sharpening me, guys. I am very grateful to have you in my life.

To Larissa Salazar, Mel New, and John Kruger: My peer edit team! Thank you so much for sharing your honest feedback on this book, at the risk of sometimes making this author uncomfortable. It was worth it. This book is much better because of you.

To Kim Louie Lapidante: Thank you for so consistently supporting me on this project. Your work in support of this book was monumental, and I cannot send you enough praise. Thank you!

To single Christians everywhere: I pray that this book brings you hope, life, and a dose of encouragement. More importantly, I pray that it points you to Life Himself.

And lastly, to my family: Words cannot express my gratitude for you. I feel like the luckiest son and brother that this world has known. I love you with all that I am.

God bless you all,

ENDNOTES

THE PAULINE ADVANTAGE

1   C. S. Lewis, *An Experiment in Criticism* (Cambridge University Press, 1961), 141.

2   Eric Metaxas, *Bonhoeffer: Pastor, Martyr, Prophet, Spy* (Thomas Nelson, 2010), 70.

3   Metaxas, *Bonhoeffer*, 183.

4   Metaxas, *Bonhoeffer*, 183.

DAY ONE – YOUR GOD

5   Joshua Noble, "Titanic Religious Services and Hymnology," *Titanic Legacy*, published November 21, 2024, https://www.titaniclegacy.us/titanic-articles/titanic-religious-services-and-hymnology.

6   Louisa M. R. Stead, "'Tis So Sweet to Trust in Jesus," in *African American Heritage Hymnal* (GIA Publications, 2001), 368.

DAY TWO – YOUR SELF

7   C. S. Lewis, *Mere Christianity* (HarperOne, 2001), 49.

DAY FOUR – YOUR FRIENDS

8   C. S. Lewis, *The Four Loves* (Harcourt, Brace, 1960), 73.

DAY EIGHT - YOUR CHURCH

9   Abbott Kahler, "The Daredevil of Niagara Falls," *Smithsonian Magazine*, October 18, 2011, https://www.smithsonianmag.com/history/the-daredevil-of-niagara-falls-110492884/.

DAY NINE - YOUR WORLD

10   C. S. Lewis, *Mere Christianity* (HarperOne, 2001), 155.

11   Chris Roberts, "How Cannabis Accidentally Helped Reopen Churches During the COVID Pandemic," *Forbes*, August 26, 2020, https://www.forbes.com/sites/chrisroberts/2020/08/26/how-cannabis-accidentally-helped-reopen-churches-during-the-covid-pandemic/.

12   Mary Margaret Olohan and Leif Le Mahieu, "President Trump to Pardon Imprisoned Pro-Life Activists Within Days," *The Daily Wire*, January 23, 2025, https://www.dailywire.com/news/president-trump-to-pardon-imprisoned-pro-life-activists-within-days.

DAY TEN - YOUR SIN

13   C. S. Lewis, *Mere Christianity* (HarperOne, 2001), 31.

DAY ELEVEN - YOUR PRIDE

14   C. S. Lewis, *Mere Christianity* (HarperOne, 2001), 122.

15   F. B. Meyer, quoted in Andrew Murray, *Humility* (Whitaker House, 2001), 95.

DAY TWELVE - YOUR PAIN

16   C. S. Lewis, *The Problem of Pain* (HarperOne, 2001), 31.

DAY FOURTEEN - YOUR LONELINESS

17   C. S. Lewis, *The Four Loves* (HarperOne, 2012), 2.

18   Elisabeth Elliot, *Passion and Purity: Learning to Bring Your Love Life Under Christ's Control* (Revell, 2002), 79, 81.

DAY FIFTEEN – YOUR FAITH

19 George Müller, *The Autobiography of George Müller* (Whitaker House, 1984), 13, 15.

20 Müller, *The Autobiography of George Müller*, 37.

21 Müller, *The Autobiography of George Müller*, 37.

DAY SEVENTEEN – YOUR HOPES AND DREAMS

22 Derek Prince, *Secrets of a Prayer Warrior* (Chosen Books, 2009), 1.

23 C. S. Lewis, *Mere Christianity* (New York: HarperOne, 2001), 135.

24 Elisabeth Elliot, *Passion and Purity: Learning to Bring Your Love Life Under Christ's Control* (Revell, 2002), 89.

DAY EIGHTEEN – YOUR MUSIC AND MEDIA

25 Smithsonian Institution, Butterflies, Information Sheet Number 168, prepared by the Department of Systematic Biology, Entomology Section, National Museum of Natural History, in cooperation with Public Inquiry Services, Smithsonian Institution, 1996, accessed March 28, 2025, https://www.si.edu/spotlight/buginfo/butterfly.

26 Edwin Louis Cole, *Maximized Manhood* (Whitaker House, 2001), 129.

27 Quote attributed to Blaise Pascal: "It's not those who write the laws that have the greatest impact on society. It's those who write the songs." Attribution disputed.

DAY NINETEEN – YOUR SPEECH

28 George Washington, "General Orders, 3 August 1775," Founders Online, National Archives, https://founders.archives.gov/documents/Washington/03-05-02-0415. Originally published in *The Papers of George Washington, Revolutionary War Series*, vol. 5, 16 June 1776–12 August 1776, ed. Philander D. Chase (University Press of Virginia, 1993), 551–552.

DAY TWENTY – YOUR SILENCE

29 Alexandre Dumas, *The Count of Monte Cristo* (Barnes & Noble Classics, 2011), 128.

30 Dumas, *The Count of Monte Cristo*, 128.

31   EBSCO, "Letters and Papers from Prison by Dietrich Bonhoeffer," EBSCO Research Starters, accessed March 29, 2025. https://www.ebsco.com/ research-starters/literature-and-writing/letters-and-papers-prison-dietrich-bonhoeffer.

32   J. Oswald Sanders, quoted in Dave Buehring, *A Discipleship Journey* (Lionshare, 2009), 17.

33   John Mark Comer, *The Ruthless Elimination of Hurry* (WaterBrook, 2019), 130.

34   Martin Luther, quoted in George Grant, "Normal Prayer," Ligonier Ministries, March 31, 2003, accessed March 29, 2025, https://learn. ligonier.org/articles/normal-prayer.

DAY TWENTY-ONE – YOUR OBEDIENCE

35   C. S. Lewis, *Mere Christianity* (HarperOne, 2001), 205, 206.

DAY TWENTY-FOUR – YOUR WORK

36   Timothy Keller, *Every Good Endeavor: Connecting Your Work to God's Plan for the World* (Dutton, 2012), 21.

DAY TWENTY-SIX – YOUR APPEARANCE

37   "Women in Bathing Suits Being Arrested," Encyclopedia.com, accessed April 1, 2025. https://www.encyclopedia.com/law/educational-magazines/. women-bathing-suits-being-arrested.

38   C. S. Lewis, *The Four Loves* (New York: HarperOne, 2012), 121.

DAY TWENTY-SEVEN – YOUR FOOD

39   Randy Alcorn, *Heaven* (Tyndale House Publishers, 2004), 307.

40   Fred Bahnson, *Making Peace with the Land* (IVP Books, 2012), 63, quoted in Josh Bishop, "Digesting Grace: Why the Food We Eat Matters to God," *Christianity Today*, August 15, 2012, https://www.christianitytoday. com/2012/08/digesting-grace/.

DAY TWENTY-EIGHT – YOUR SEXUALITY

41   "Purity Ring," *Wikipedia*, last modified July 10, 2025, https://en.wikipedia. org/wiki/Purity_ring.

DAY THIRTY – YOUR FUTURE

42   Dietrich Bonhoeffer, "Who Am I?" in *Bonhoeffer: Pastor, Martyr, Prophet, Spy* by Eric Metaxas (Thomas Nelson, 2010), in photo section between 464 and 465.

43   Walks in Rome, "The Church of San Paolo alle Tre Fontane in Rome," Walks in Rome, accessed March 29, 2025, https://www.walksinrome.com/the-church-of-san-paolo-alle-tre-fontane-in-rome.html.

44   Origen, as quoted in *Eusebius, The Ecclesiastical History*, trans. Kirsopp Lake, vol. 1 (Harvard University Press, 1926), book 3, chapter 1.

45   United States Holocaust Memorial Museum, "Dietrich Bonhoeffer," Holocaust Encyclopedia, accessed March 29, 2025, https://encyclopedia.ushmm.org/content/en/article/dietrich-bonhoeffer.